Zen & Karma

Zen & Karma

Teachings by Roshi Taisen Deshimaru

Edited by Rei Ryu Philippe Coupey
Revised Edition, *The Voice of the Valley*

HOHM PRESS
Chino Valley, Arizona

© 2016, Zen Association, Philippe Coupey
All rights reserved. No part of this book may be reproduced in any manner without written permission from the publisher, except in the case of quotes used in critical articles and reviews.

Cover Design: Adi Zuccarello, www.adizuccarello.com
Interior Design and Layout: Becky Fulker, Kubera Book Design, Prescott, AZ
Calligraphy by Taisen Deshimaru Roshi
Calligraphy on front cover by Françoise Lesage

Library of Congress Cataloging-in-Publication Data

Names: Deshimaru, Taisen, author. | Coupey, Philippe, editor.
Title: Zen & karma : teachings by Roshi Taisen Deshimaru / edited by Rei Ryu Philippe Coupey.
Other titles: Voice of the valley
Description: Chino Valley, Arizona : Hohm Press, 2016. | Revised edition of: The voice of the valley : Indianapolis : Bobbs-Merrill, "1979. | Includes index.
Identifiers: LCCN 2016007176 | ISBN 9781942493143 (trade pbk. : alk. paper)
Subjects: LCSH: Zen Buddhism–Sermons. | Buddhist sermons, English.
Classification: LCC BQ9435.D47 V64 2016 | DDC 294.3/420427–dc23
LC record available at http://lccn.loc.gov/2016007176

Hohm Press
P.O. Box 4410
Chino Valley, AZ 86323
800-381-2700
http://www.hohmpress.com

This book was printed in the U.S.A. on recycled, acid-free paper using soy ink.

Original copyright © 1979 by Taisen Deshimaru Roshi; published by The Bobbs Merrill Company, Inc. New York
Library of Congress Cataloging in Publication Data
Deshimaru, Taisen.
The voice of the valley.
Includes index.
1. Sotoshu-ons. 2. Buddhist sermons, English.
I. Coupey, Philippe. II. Title.
BQ943S.D47V64   294.3'4   78-11207
ISBN 0-672-52520-8
ISBN 0-672-52586-0 pbk.

Photo Credits: Copyright on all photos : Association Zen Internationale (AZI) except, *With Native-American Chiefs*, copyright Philippe Coupey. *With the kyosaku* by J.C. Varga

I prostrate myself in sampai
Before the Three treasures
The Buddha, the Dharma and the Sangha.
And I prostrate myself in sampai
Before my Master Taisen Deshimaru.

—Philippe Rei Ryu Coupey

Acknowledgements

I would like to thank Jonas Endres, Marie Gaspar, Olivier Tollu and Maddie Parisio for their help.

Calligraphy by Taisen Deshimaru Roshi: "Mountain and River"

Contents

Note to the Reader xiii
Foreword by Yoko Orimo xv
Introduction to the Second Edition by Philippe Coupey xix
Line of the Transmission .... xxiv-xxv

Session 1
    The secret of zazen 3
    The voice and the posture of Buddha 4
    Passions and illusions 5
    Understanding Zen 6
    "Good" and "bad" are human words 8
    Transmigration and reincarnation 9
    Returning to the root 10
    Forgetting the ego 12

Session 2
    Letting go of thoughts 17
    Living without calculating 18
    One kesa, one poem 20
    Looking at one's karma before the final hour 21
    Getting past attachment 22
    Yesterday's ego is not today's 23
    The flame of our actions continues 25
    Body and cosmos are not separate 25
    Karma, like the ego is without substance 27
    A new humanity 29
    What is true happiness? 30
    Karma is not fatalism 33
    Becoming truly free 36
    Nothing other than existence 38
    Karma, causality… and beyond 39
    Ten thousand causes, ten thousand effects 41
    Our existence cannot be seen in isolation 42
    Interdependence, a two-way road 44
    Mondo (Questions and Answers) 47

ZEN & KARMA

    The living nirvana 48
    Mistaken methods 50
    What always endures 52
    Mondo (Questions and Answers) 53
    The soul 55
    Confidence in the satori of Buddha 57

Session 3

    Beyond meditation 63
    Thinking in the depths of non-thinking 64
    Ku, our original nature 66
    Realization within the everyday world 67
    Transforming illusions 69
    A strong education 71
    About cause and effect: not so obvious 72
    Behavior and consciousness 74
    Zazen, objectively certified? 76
    Karma, a subjective problem 78
    A poem to go beyond language 79
    Understanding the conditions of our existence 81
    Merits beyond gain and loss 81
    Karma produces nothing of itself 82
    Non-manifested karma is like a seed 83
    Zazen's influence on karma 85
    When a tree falls its shadow disappears 87
    Cutting the root of karma 88
    Non-manifested karma 91
    Nature, action and the cosmic order 94
    Transforming the ego, is that possible? 96
    Seeking the true religion (Nembutsu, Christianity, Zen…) .. 98
    Mondo (Questions and Answers) 97
    Mu, when the ego is abandoned 101
    "Good causes, good effects": not axiomatic 104
    Manual work rather than manuals 105
    Behavior influences civilization 107
    Training the body-mind 109
    Observing one's karma 110
    Mondo (Questions and Answers) 112

Session 4

Exact sitting	115
A sesshin is absolutely necessary	117
Karma repeats itself	118
A tree knows neither happiness nor unhappiness	120
Right posture influences everyone else	121
Without fear, free	122
Neither strange nor miraculous	124
A physical education	125
Complete communion	126
Do not neglect the body	128
God has no need of conversation	130
When consciousness becomes physical	130
Mondo (Questions and Answers)	134
Stages?	132
One point in the cosmic system	141
Do not move, neither with the body nor the mind	142
Theology without practice is empty	144
Stronger, kyosaku!	146
God is in our minds, not in the sky	149
Training oneself in patience	152
Mondo (Questions and Answers)	155
"I believe more in the Bible than in the sutras…"	158
A strong practice is necessary	160
Ideas of time	161
The posture of zazen is the true living Buddha	163
Satori is not important	166
A koan in solid bronze	167

Appendix by Philippe Coupey: *Changing Your Karma*	171
Glossary	175
Index	189
About Taisen Deshimaru	200
About the Editor	202
Contact Information	202

Note to the Reader

The present work is the fully reviewed and corrected edition of a book that initially appeared in 1979 in the United States under the title of *The Voice of the Valley* (published by Bobbs-Merrill), then later in France, and in other European languages.

The book is compiled from the oral teachings (*kusen*) given by Master Deshimaru during zazen, and questions and answers (*mondo*) with the master drawn from the notes taken by his disciple and scribe Philippe Coupey during the summer retreat of 1977 in the Val d'Isère in France.

Master Deshimaru upheld the tradition established by Shakyamuni Buddha of a long "sesshin," summer retreat, of about two months, during which an intensive practice of meditation was blended with all the tasks necessary for life together as a sangha.

The editorial choice of the original version (*The Voice of the Valley*) had been to present the collection of kusen, given by Master Deshimaru during this retreat, while maintaining as much as possible his lively oral characteristics and power of his teachings. Taisen Deshimaru was a man of free ideas and strong words, and the remarkable success of this book is that the text, having been through transcription and presentation, still remains true to the movement of his words and the singular sound of his voice.

The four sessions of the summer camp in this book took place almost forty years ago. Obviously, the situation at the time of the first publication is quite different from the present day. This has developed the evolution of its presentation into a new, clearer form, which addresses not only the practitioners in Master Deshimaru's sangha, but everyone wishing to know the meaning of karma.

It should be pointed out that, apart from the indications regarding the body and mind during meditation and some passages clearly manifesting the master's sense of humor and taste for anecdotes, you will find herein a memorable teaching of great force that requires the full attention of the reader in order to take part in Master Deshimaru's vision, since he uses words which, in the cosmic order, are implacably in the domain of the apophatic.

Foreword

by Yoko Orimo

The original title of this book *The Voice of the Valley* (*Keisei*) is taken from *Keisei Sanshoku* (the voice of the valleys, the color-shapes of the mountains), fascicle 25 of the *Shobogenzo*. It is a collected series of *kusen* (short group instruction) and *mondo* (public exchange between master and disciple) given by Taisen Deshimaru during the summer retreat at Val d'Isère, France, from July 25th to August 31st 1977, a total of thirty-seven days divided into four sessions or camps.

"Freshness" and "dynamism": these are the two words that I would use to describe this beautiful book. How often does the phrase "the fundamental cosmic power" issue from the mouth of the Japanese master with an energy whose target is to introduce Europeans to the practice of *zazen*? "*Push the sky with your head and the ground with your knees*" is his chosen formula to describe the seated posture. "*What is Satori (awakening)?*" To this question the master replies. "*There's no need to seek it; zazen itself is Satori.*" The magnificent calligraphy, that sets the rhythm for this volume, brings to mind the strength of Deshimaru's fiery and vigorous personality. Is it intentional on his part that we see on the inside cover the Japanese word for "mountains and rivers," which is pronounced *sanga*, a homonym for the Sanskrit term *sangha*, the "community of practitioners"?

In simple language accessible to everyone, Deshimaru expounds upon the fundamental ideas of Buddhist doctrine, taking for his material the practical and concrete issues of our daily lives. In the background throughout appear, on the one hand, Deshimaru's deep roots in his own Japanese culture and, on the other, his vast knowledge of—I would go so far as to say, his love affair with—the West, going beyond the confessional or religious setting. I was delighted, for example to find Kenji

Miyazawa's poem, which I too learned by heart as a schoolgirl, since it's an anthem, almost a national anthem, exalting lay Buddhist spirituality to its peak. At the same time, the names of Western poets, philosophers and scientists are sprinkled everywhere, liberally cited by the Japanese master in the light of his Zen teaching. I was astonished to find him speaking so freely of God and Christianity. I have the feeling of having met a true "spiritual friend" (zen.nu) especially since, in today's European practitioners, I see nothing but the almost systematic rejection of everything relating to the Christian tradition, for the sake of doctrinal "purity" which should consist, according to them, in protecting Buddhism from being at all influenced by a European heritage that is more than two thousand years old: an endeavor which is, in my opinion, doomed to fail. How can European practitioners realize Awakening (Satori) if they sweep away their own tradition and their own identity? It's as if the Japanese, Buddhist or not, were to reject their Buddhist heritage and disown their tradition and identity.

I never knew Deshimaru in his lifetime. However, from a number of his direct disciples I have heard all kinds of appraisals and comments. If some express their deep attachment, both emotional and spiritual, there are others who criticize, either with a hard dry tongue or with a light smile. Malicious tongues say that Deshimaru was not a great master, he simply profited from the 1968 protest movement and trends to gather his assortment of disciples. Let us remember, however, the undeniable fact that if Zen is now transmitted on European soil, it is thanks to Deshimaru personally, not to any institution. So how could the name of Taisen Deshimaru be struck from the genealogical proceedings of the law (*shisho*); how could Zen practitioners leave this first European patriarch without a successor?

Some people point to his private life before his departure from Japan, which was admittedly not exemplary; moreover he smoked and liked good French wine. Personally, I'm not looking to him for the image of a venerable saint. I simply feel a deep sympathy, even a certain affinity with this characterful missionary.

Foreword

Driven by the sole desire to spread Zen across the European land of which he dreamed, he travelled to France alone in 1967 on the Trans-Siberian railroad. He had no resources in the beginning and earned a modest day-to-day living by offering *shiatsu* (therapeutic Japanese massage) and from the takings of a tiny macrobiotic store, receiving no financial aid. I see no political calculation, no personal ambition, nothing but the burning apostolic heart of a true missionary.

It was also Deshimaru who transmitted to Europe a love and passion for the *Shobogenzo*, "The true Law, the Treasure of the Eye." He did not speak French. His teaching, given in broken English, was translated by his disciples who were probably as ignorant of Buddhist doctrine as they were of the Japanese language. I quite understand the judicious criticism by today's connoisseurs of his rather too free and fragmentary "translation" of the *Shobogenzo*, a "translation" which has now been eclipsed. However, here once again, is what really counts in my eyes: this Japanese missionary loved the *Treasure* passionately, not as an erudite philologist, nor as a professor of Buddhism, nor as a monk mandated to teach by the establishment, but as a free man with no academic pretensions, existentially steeped in this *Treasure* of the heart and mind.

More than thirty-five years after its first publication, this book shows no sign of age. However, present-day Buddhism in Europe, in the form of Soto Zen might not be aging so well. The wish to institutionalize the different existing elements could reintroduce formalism along with a ritualism that is cut off from reality, the more or less fictitious lineage of master and disciple, etc. Soon, the first generation of Deshimaru's disciples must pass. For the sake of the European Zen of the future, would it not be good if practitioners took to the open sea with a great fondness for Deshimaru as their sail, receiving the study of the *Shobogenzo* like the breath of a fair wind?

—Yoko Orimo

Director of the Institute of Buddhist studies in Paris. Author and translator, graduated from *L'école pratique des Hautes Etudes* in Paris, specialist in the *Shobogenzo* by Master Dogen.

Introduction to the Second Edition

A word on karma

The subject of this book is karma. Karma is the action (the motion, the movement) of body, mind and speech. What we are today, what we think and what we do, *depends* upon how this our body and this our mind, was in the past; likewise, what we will become today and tomorrow and forevermore, *depends* upon how this body and mind are today in the here-and-now. Also, it is said that human beings must learn to change this karma, to free themselves from it; to free themselves from the karmic law of action and reaction, from its nets and snares of delusion. In other words, we must learn *how* to act, and to act from within.

A word on the setting

This book records Taisen Deshimaru's kusens (teachings), other comments and answers to questions made during four one-week-long sesshins, or meditation retreats, in the summer of 1977. Meditation retreats in summer date from Buddha's times and are still considered the most important occasion to practice the Way for longer periods all together in the sangha, the community of practitioners.

During the three or four zazen periods per day we sat in rows, one behind the other, four and five deep. Beyond the large French windows some snow-capped mountains could be seen, and the mountain river Isère could be heard rushing beneath the dojo. According to custom, the master was seated to the right of the entrance, and to the left sat the four *kyosakumen*.[1] Directly

---

[1] The *kyosaku* is the "wake-up stick" and four of them were necessary in order to monitor the 200 practitioners or more seated in the dojo at that time.

to the right of the master sat the spontaneous translator. Next in line sat the secretary, and then the transcribers, one of them writing the teaching down in French, the other (myself, an American) in the original English.

Besides zazen, life was concentrated on *samu*, working for the sangha. We ate together in silence, but Deshimaru never was against conversation outside of the dojo or the dining hall. We even had, and still have, festive activities in between the one-week-sessions; we created theatre, music and parties. It was up to each one of us to be attentive and refrain from making these activities trivial.

Taisen Deshimaru

Taisen Deshimaru was born off the coast of southern Japan, on the island of Kyushu, in 1914. He was raised by his grandfather, who was a samurai master before the Meiji Revolution, and by his mother, a devout follower of the Buddhist Shinshu sect. Whatever the circumstances of his upbringing and his education (he graduated from the University of Yokohama), Deshimaru was greatly tormented by what he called the ephemeral world of birth and death; and it was in this context that he began to study the Christian Bible. He continued thus for many years under the guidance of a Protestant minister, with whom he had developed strong bonds. This search for understanding and for peace of mind led him eventually to Zen, first under the guidance of Master Asahina of the Rinzai School, then under Master Kodo Sawaki of the Soto school. With Kodo Sawaki it became clear that his search for a master was over, and he stayed with him until the latter's death in 1965.

However, with the Japanese attack on Pearl Harbor in December 1941, their world changed overnight, and disciple and master had to part company. "We will certainly lose the war," said Sawaki. "Our homeland will be destroyed and our people annihilated...; this may be the last time we see one another. But whatever happens, love all mankind regardless of race or creed."

With his country at war, Deshimaru was employed, not as a soldier but as a businessman directing a copper mining company

Introduction to the Second Edition

on the island of Bangka, off the coast of Sumatra. Meanwhile, the people of Bangka, most of whom were of Chinese extraction, were undergoing indescribably brutal persecution at the hands of the Japanese invaders, and Deshimaru interfered on their behalf. He was eventually arrested by the Imperial Army and sentenced to death by a firing squad. However, directly before his execution was to take place, the order arrived from the highest military authorities in Tokyo to set the man free (though the reason for this last minute acquittal was never made clear, either it was because his family and friends had good connections back home, or simply because of he himself and his bright star in the sky).

When the war came to an end, Deshimaru was again taken prisoner, this time by the Americans. He was incarcerated for many long months in a prisoner-of-war camp in Singapore. First incarcerated by the Japanese, then by the Americans, decidedly, Deshimaru represented a serious snag in the apparatus, be it Japanese or American, politics or ambition or whatever; and so too it was in his relationship to the Zen establishment. He left Japan, partly because of this deep-seated divergence of mind and vision that he had with those in authority, in any authority. And he didn't go to the United States, also for this reason. He went to France. (Again, and for no anodyne reason, this particular book, first published by Bobbs-Merrill in 1979 with the title *The Voice of the Valley*, was refused distribution in the States, and its entire stock was quickly disposed of. In fact, it became "forbidden reading" in many of the American Zen centers—the reasons for which the attentive reader will in due time discover for him- or herself). Upon his release from the prisoner of war camp, Deshimaru rejoined Kodo Sawaki and, as noted above, he remained there until the latter's death fourteen years later.

Deshimaru buried his master's skull in the ground outside the temple of Antaiji and then sat in zazen for forty-nine days. Breaking away from the roots in his homeland and from the Japanese Soto Zen hierarchy (and at the same time leaving behind his wife and children), he departed alone for Russia and Europe.

He settled in France and remained there; and it was from there that he spread the Dharma like no one else before him.

~

Deshimaru arrived in Europe in 1967, unannounced and unexpected, not connected to any organization, religious or otherwise; and working for no one but himself (initially as a masseur), having no one to report back to, he was free to act as he wished. And so he did. In the fifteen years left of his life, Sensei (as he preferred to be called), established a basis upon which Zen could thrive in the West, a Zen void of useless Japanese ceremony, hierarchy, grades and other protocol. Having settled far away from the *Sotoshu* and the *Shumucho* headquarters in Tokyo, he could bring to the European continent the excellent and unadulterated practice of *shikantaza* without grades and with nothing else attached.[2]

Deshimaru was a very spontaneous man; he was joyful, and he was angry—joyful with life, and yet angry with his disciples who did not find the Satori he would have wished for them. But he was not a severe man, and he imposed no restrictions on anyone. You could do as you wished. "*Faites comme vous voulez*" [Do as you like], he would say in French. In the dojo, however, you practiced only zazen and kinhin. "Zen is only zazen," he used to say and this is what he practiced every day. Yet, shortly before that retreat in Val d'Isère was to begin, Sensei asked me to write down his teaching in the dojo. I protested saying that I didn't want to write during the practice, I just wanted to do zazen, that's all. He replied: "Zazen is not important."

It was always about going beyond one's concepts and limitations. One day at a sesshin, he asked one of his close

---

[2] Even the grade of *kyoshi* now in use with most Shumucho affiliates in France and in the States consists of many rungs, like rungs on a ladder, the first rung being the grade of *nitokyoshi* and given to the sons of temple abbots, while the highest rung on this same ladder being *Dai-kyosei* given with pomp and ceremony to the *zenjis* of Eihei-ji or Soji-ji.

disciples to call up the French Air Force, to ask them to stop the test flights they were running just above the dojo. When the disciple in question called up the Air Force, they immediately stopped and excused themselves for having run test flights out of the authorized hours.

World consciousness
Sensei was always telling us to sit without object, without goal. To be beyond personal thoughts. This is what he taught and, "To think from the bottom of not-thinking"[3] was one of the many expressions of his own making. But for this to come about, self-knowledge is essential. He said it this way: "to understand oneself is to understand the universe. The microcosm and the macrocosm are one. Evolution always begins with the individual; and if a man takes one step forward, he carries the world consciousness one step forward."

In order to implement this teaching, Deshimaru put particular emphasis on the seated posture, with knees planted firmly on the ground, the spinal column naturally erect, the neck too, with head held straight and pressing upward against the sky. The shoulders down and relaxed, with the hands resting palms upwards and against the belly, under the navel. And the same emphasis on the kinhin posture of zazen in motion as well. And so with the breathing. The exhalation deep and long, the inhalation short and steady. The ability to control our body and mind, and to change our lives, to change our karma, he would say, depends upon this breathing; on our ability to concentrate on the breathing, on the out-breath. This is what he always said. And too, he would point out that all schools of Buddhism agree that *anapanasati* (awareness of the breathing) was the Buddha Shakyamuni's first teaching.

—Philippe Rei Ryu Coupey
Paris, 21/10/2015

---

[3] And not "non-thinking" which was too theoretical for the master's liking.

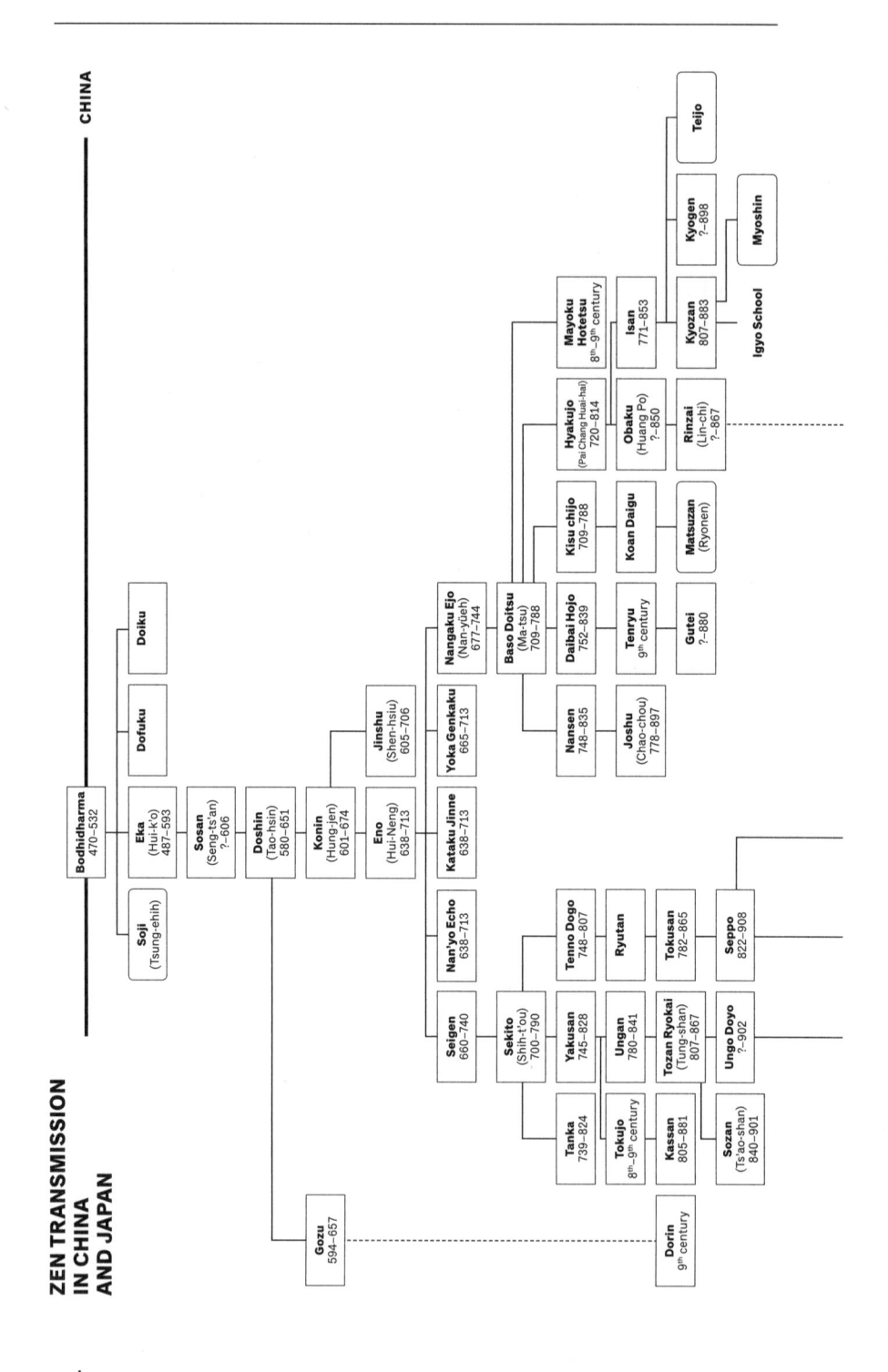

ZEN & KARMA

ZEN TRANSMISSION IN CHINA AND JAPAN

- Bodhidharma 470–532
  - Soji (Tsung-ehih)
  - Eka (Hui-k'o) 487–593
    - Dofuku
    - Doiku
    - Sosan (Seng-ts'an) ?–606
      - Doshin (Tao-hsin) 580–651
        - Konin (Hung-jen) 601–674
          - Jinshu (Shen-hsiu) 605–706
          - Eno (Hui-Neng) 638–713
            - Yoka Genkaku 665–713
            - Kataku Jinne 638–713
            - Nangaku Ejo (Nan-yüeh) 677–744
              - Mayoku Hotetsu 8th–9th century
              - Baso Doitsu (Ma-tsu) 709–788
                - Hyakujo (Pai Chang Huai-hai) 720–814
                  - Obaku (Huang Po) ?–850
                    - Rinzai (Lin-chi) ?–867
                - Kisu chijo 709–788
                - Daibai Hojo 752–839
                - Nansen 748–835
                - Koan Daigu
                - Tenryu 9th century
                  - Gutei ?–880
                - Joshu (Chao-chou) 778–897
                - Matsuzan (Ryonen)
              - Isan 771–853
                - Kyozan 807–883
                  - Kyogen ?–898
                    - Teijo
                  - Myoshin
                - Igyo School
            - Nan'yo Echo 638–713
            - Seigen 660–740
              - Sekito (Shih-t'ou) 700–790
                - Tanka 739–824
                - Tenno Dogo 748–807
                  - Ryutan
                    - Tokusan 782–865
                      - Seppo 822–908
                - Yakusan 745–828
                  - Tokujo 8th–9th century
                  - Ungan 780–841
                    - Tozan Ryokai (Tung-shan) 807–867
                      - Kassan 805–881
                      - Ungo Doyo ?–902
                        - Sozan (Ts'ao-shan) 840–901
  - Gozu 594–657
    - Dorin 9th century

CHINA

Introduction to the Second Edition

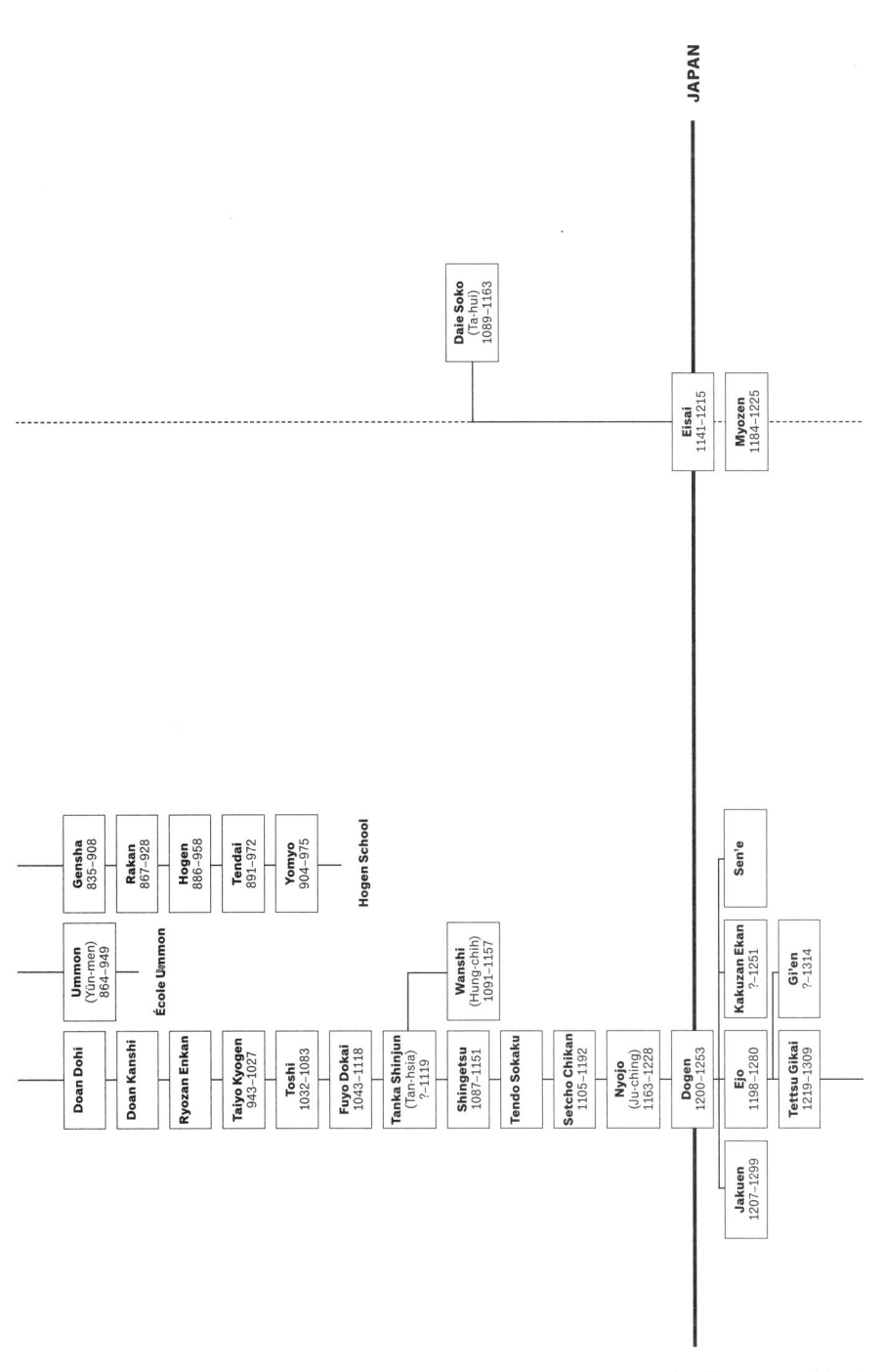

JAPAN

- Daie Soko (Ta-hui) 1089–1163
- Eisai 1141–1215
- Myozen 1184–1225

- Gensha 835–908
- Rakan 867–928
- Hogen 886–958
- Tendai 891–972
- Yomyo 904–975
- Hogen School

- Ummon (Yün-men) 864–949
- École Ummon
- Wanshi (Hung-chih) 1091–1157
- Sen'e

- Doan Dohi
- Doan Kanshi
- Ryozan Enkan
- Taiyo Kyogen 943–1027
- Toshi 1032–1083
- Fuyo Dokai 1043–1118
- Tanka Shinjun (Tan-hsia) ?–1119
- Shingetsu 1087–1151
- Tendo Sokaku
- Setcho Chikan 1105–1192
- Nyojo (Ju-ching) 1163–1228
- Dogen 1200–1253
- Ejo 1198–1280
- Tettsu Gikai 1219–1309
- Kakuzan Ekan ?–1251
- Gi'en ?–1314

- Jakuen 1207–1299

(continues on next page)

xxv

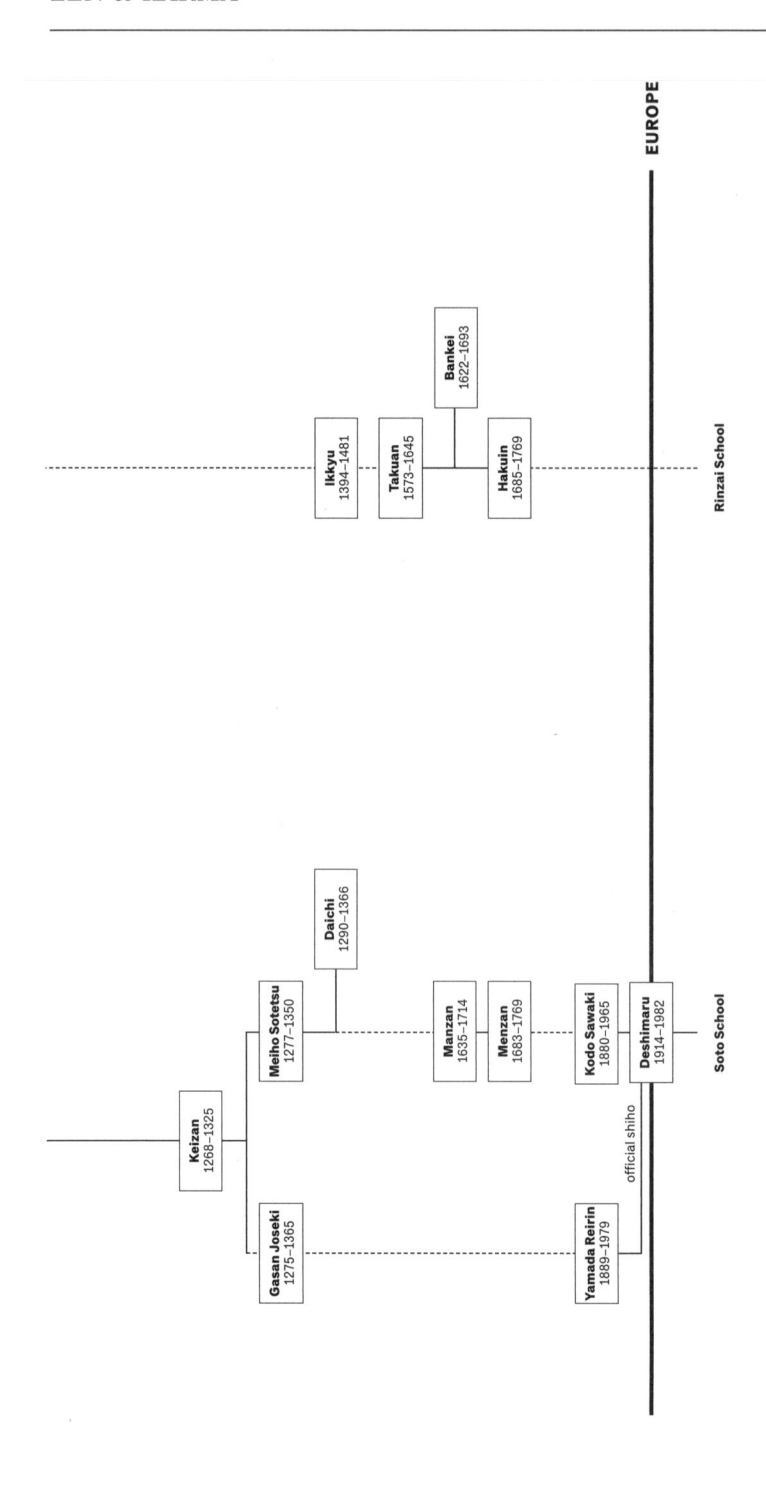

ZEN & KARMA

Ikkyu 1394–1481

Takuan 1573–1645

Bankei 1622–1693

Hakuin 1685–1769

Rinzai School

Keizan 1268–1325

Gasan Joseki 1275–1365

Meiho Sotetsu 1277–1350

Daichi 1290–1366

Manzan 1635–1714

Menzan 1683–1769

Kodo Sawaki 1880–1965

Yamada Reirin 1889–1979

Deshimaru 1914–1982

official shiho

Soto School

EUROPE

Note: The rectangles with rounded corners represent women.
This tree of transmission is taken from the versions drawn up by Masters Kodo Sawaki and Taisen Deshimaru. Ph. C, Rei Ryu 99/revised in 2015.

xxvi

OPPOSITE: *Hishiryo*—Beyond thinking, absolute thinking

Session One

July 27 – July 30, 1977

The secret of zazen

In the *Fukanzazengi*[1] by Master Dogen it is written as follows: "Please, think Hishiryo—non-thinking. How do we think non-thinking? Hishiryo is beyond thinking; Hishiryo is absolute thinking. This is the important secret of zazen."

Hishiryo includes all things, all existences, the good and the bad, the relative and the absolute, the rational and the irrational. Hishiryo is non-egoistic. It is cosmic thinking.

The cosmic order is not, as modern-day physicists are now pointing out, merely rationalistic. These prominent physicists are now in agreement that sometimes the cosmic order (the cosmic system) destroys, sometimes it creates. Sometimes for the good, sometimes for the bad. That, namely, it includes all contradictions. And if you do not follow the cosmic order, your life will be difficult.

During zazen you can become Hishiryo automatically, unconsciously and naturally.

~

We must understand that from within the relationship between the fundamental cosmic power and one's personal, subjective existence arises the fundamental source of karma.

Fundamental cosmic power has no beginning and no end. It is beyond time and space. It does not have to do with personal choice, for this power directs man from the outside. Even if we imagine that we are completely free, thanks to our own willpower, this is not so. We can never separate ourselves from the cosmic system. Willpower itself is realized from within this fundamental cosmic power.

---

[1] *Fukanzazengi*: A work dealing with the practical rules of zazen. See Glossary.

We are at times directed by the frontal brain—and this is self-will, self-thinking. At other times we are directed by the fundamental cosmic power. When our will is opposed to the cosmic power, we become attached to our own personal bonnos.[2] At such times our body-action, our body-karma, as well as our personal consciousness, arises, and so we become governed by our personal willpower, by our inner bonnos. In Buddhism this is called *Mana-consciousness*.

I now compare passion and bonno, as explained in European and in Oriental philosophy. In *Les Passions de l'Ame*, written in 1645, Descartes separates passion from reason, and furthermore he separates them from the body. Passion, writes Descartes, arises from a state of surprise, from admiration, from that which is outside the body. In Oriental philosophy it is stated that passions—that is, bonnos—arise from within the body. In Buddhism bonnos are regarded as arising from ignorance, from the mind of ignorance.

The voice and the posture of Buddha
When the macrocosm and the microcosm harmonize within the body, and particularly within the brain, we can obtain the great energy of the macrocosm. At this moment, here in this Dojo, the energy of the macrocosm is entering into the microcosm. Through zazen we can obtain this energy, which is not simply strength—it is the energy of the infinite. This energy of which I speak is a force both spiritual and material. It has the power both of harmony and of destruction. The cosmos in itself includes these two opposite and contradictory forces.

---

[2] *Bonno: Bon* means troublesome, *no* means suffering. Thus, a desire, a passion, an illusion. See Glossary.

Session One: July 27 – July 30, 1977

The first sesshin is now beginning, and surely in these next two days you will be capable of obtaining this cosmic power. Especially here in this Dojo, with the beautiful mountains and the sound of the flowing river.

Master Dogen said that the color of the mountain, the sound of the valley—all this, everything—is the voice and the posture of Shakyamuni Buddha.

Sotoba, a famous Bodhisattva and a great writer of old China, got *Satori*[3] through the *Keishei-sanshoku*. Kei means the valley, *shei* is the sound, and *sanshoku* is the color of the mountain. The sound of the valley is giving a great conference.[4] The color of the mountain is the true, purified body. From midnight to sunrise I hear 84,000 sutra-poems. How can I explain this to others? How can I explain such a religious impression?

Val d'Isére means the river in the valley. A good name for zazen.

Passions and illusions

I will continue this kusen on the comparison between passion and bonno.

In the philosophy of Descartes, passion and reason are separated. In Buddhism they are both bonnos. The intellect too is a bonno. In certain sutras it is said that in one day people think up to two million bonnos. Each thought creates karma, and it is this which lead you into *Naraka*.[5]

Descartes deals with the problem of attachment. He writes that attachment will come to an end once the ego is abandoned. This is all he has to say on this subject. In describing desire, Descartes goes into methods for curing its negative aspects. He does not speak of zazen. He uses scientific intellectual thought, and so he deals with desire by separating it from the body.

---

[3] *Satori*: Awakening. The return to Original Mind. See Glossary.
[4] The original title of this book was *The Voice of the Valley*.
[5] *Naraka*: Hell.

Descartes always separates mind and body. He did not know about body-thinking.

If we do zazen, we can control our negative desires unconsciously, naturally and automatically.

Descartes wrote that we cannot go against our destiny—he was a fatalist. Occidental philosophy, its religions, its morals, deal with good and bad, with left and right. It is all very severe. It makes for many "isms."

In Zen, good can become bad, and bad, good. Zen includes all contradictions. The cosmic order itself is in contradiction. Science today demonstrates this point, yet Occidental thought continues to remain dualistic.

Through zazen we can see our bonnos clearly and deeply. Zen always looks into one's own mind. So through zazen we can analyze our mind, understand it, and go beyond it. We can look at the mind objectively, as if in a mirror.

We can see our bonnos objectively. This is not imagination; this is thinking, not-thinking. We can see our bonnos as if in a mirror. Let them pass, let them pass, and soon they are finished.

Hishiryo-consciousness is the mirror.

Understanding Zen

I have been reading books written by different professors in both Japan and the United States on Buddhism. Not so good. They deal only with compassion and with karma. But there are points of interest in some of these works.

Van Meter Ames, an American professor at the University of Cincinnati, writes in his *Zen and the West* that "Meditation is obviously not quite the right word in English, since it suggests thinking."

The author never experienced zazen. He has read Professor Suzuki and Alan Watts and been influenced by them—therefore, what he says is not so deep. He does not understand zazen, but he writes about it. Nonetheless, it is interesting. The author goes on to say: "This does not fit the unthinking Zen-state which the swordsman needs, the judo or karate fighter, or the sumo wrestler who must be free of intention or purpose, alert, not set but ready for anything. It would be disastrous for such a one to make up his mind about the next move. He must not think of the future before it comes, or of the past after it has passed. He must be planted fully in the present." Then he says: "Zazen is a self-contained affair with no purpose or goal beyond." This is true. He understands Zen.

Here is another point that is interesting: "The great difference between Zen and Western thought is that Zen has been pre-scientific, whereas modern science has had a central role in the West. Yet Zen, without science, even in the superstitious middle ages, completely rejected the supernaturalism of traditional Buddhism and faced life squarely on the natural level. . . .The chaos and crisis that Westerners have blundered into, they might overcome by recognizing that, though they must do without certainty—"

American Zen. Very difficult. Very complicated. Hard to understand.

"—though they must do without certainty, they have a reliable method in science, with its procedure of hypothesis and test. . . .Westerners cannot go back to pre-scientific living, but can advance to a more sensitive and Zen use of science for the common good, beyond the lure of greed and gain."

Professors are always looking at Zen objectively from the outside, so they can never really understand Zen. What is fire? The color of fire won't tell you about the fire. To know fire you must touch it. What is my happiness? My unhappiness? My bonnos? My karma? All this we understand subjectively by ourselves. Zazen is a subjective problem, not an objective one.

People who wish to receive the *kyosaku*[6] can receive it now.

---

[6] *Kyosaku*: A flat stick with which the Master or the Kyosaku-man hits the disciples on the muscles located on each shoulder near the neck. It is also known as the stick that promotes Satori, or the wake-up stick.

"Good" and "bad" are human words

What is body-action? It is body-karma. What is vocal-action? It is the karma of consciousness. These two sorts of karma-action—that of the body and that of the mouth—are influenced by our bonnos. When we express ourselves by the body or by the mouth, these movements expressed are signs of desire generated by the will. They are bonnos.

Bonnos are not merely bad, nor are they merely good. In Buddhism there are no concepts, judgments or morals concerning bonnos. Bonnos are simply dirt.

This is the opposite of the Christian concept of purity. In Christianity, purity is good, evil is bad. In Buddhism, there are no such categories. This is an important point: Good and bad are names created by man, and so they are interchangeable, and the good can become the bad, and the bad, the good, depending on time, place and custom. There is no absolute good, no absolute bad. Stones can be bad to walk on, but if you are a poet, they can be good to look at. But a stone itself is neither good nor bad. A stone is a stone; it does not become a person.

Purification and dirtiness are solely in relationship to existence. It is the same with a bonno. So the significance of a bonno is dependent upon Buddhist thought concerning psychology and desire. Desire is dirt. So too with the will. Will itself is dirt in its original nature.

From this viewpoint many problems arise. One: Since dirt is dirt, it cannot become pure. Two: How, then, can this dirt become purified? Three: Can dirt, then, become purified? Four: Dirtiness and purification are both ku—beyond.

The problem of good and bad bonnos can be resolved, depending upon the century, the milieu, the individual. But as to the problem of dirt arid purity, it cannot be resolved by personal solutions or by time. For it is beyond time, beyond even the objective principle. Cut away, throw away, even change existence itself, and still we would not solve this problem.

Action, or karma, is the realization of the fundamental cosmic power in man. If this substance of action, or of karma, becomes one with the will, the root of all movement is solved. This fundamental cosmic power can be realized within our own personal will—through zazen.

Once this is realized, once our will is directed by this cosmic force, it is no longer a question of one's own personal willpower—it is a question of Hishiryo-consciousness. Hishiryo arises unconsciously, naturally, automatically.

Transmigration and reincarnation

Since ancient times man has accepted all kinds of thoughts concerning death. Even today this question is not dealt with profoundly, particularly among the young. Life, for the young, is more interesting than death, and so they make no commentary on death. They believe only in life. This problem of death-and-after does not interest them. Even were such people actually interested in this problem, their minds—intellectual minds, substantiated by current methodological doctrines—could never be satisfied.

The connection between life and after-death arises when we reflect on our ego. Is our life real? Does it have true meaning? Only then, when we reflect in this fashion, does the question of life and of death become meaningful. When we run after food, sex and the like—when we are directed by the social system—we have no time to reflect upon ourselves. Our self-consciousness is not strong enough to allow us deep reflection upon ourselves and upon death.

We must wake ourselves up.

As to this problem of death-and-after, some say that to know about it we must die first. And they leave it at that. It is easy to speak like this, but to accept death is not so easy. It means long and deep experience and reflection. It is not the number of experiences but the intensity of the experience that is important.

Such reflection is not for others but for ourselves. It cannot be solved by scientific study, nor by methodological doctrines, objective certification, objective stories or objective religious experiences.

People who have obtained Satori through religious methods—unconsciously, naturally and automatically—have difficulty explaining this experience to others. He who has it can only tell you that you must experience it yourselves, that you must practice it yourselves.

To understand an unhappy person, and to understand his problems objectively, is not the method. To become unhappy, and to suffer with him, is the method. If we do not taste the same experience as the other, we are of no help.

So this problem of samsara, transmigration and reincarnation can be resolved only through deep reflection on death. It depends upon subjective feelings. To truly understand depends upon the reasoning done by each separate individual.

Here, now, in this Dojo, we accept the fundamental cosmic power. We receive it strongly. With only one branch in the chimney, the fire is weak. The more branches, the stronger the fire. Each one of you now has a good posture—ego is being abandoned unconsciously, automatically, naturally.

Returning to the root
Our mind is completely pure. When we think, the mind becomes complicated. So let the thoughts pass, pass, pass, and no attachment will occur.

Sometimes we must cut the branches—then we can return to the root and so become strong. There is no need to become attached. In the *Shodoka* it is written that you must not seek the leaves, nor the branches; you must return to the root.

Zazen means to return to the root.

The *Shin Jin Mei*, the *Sandokai*, the *Hokyo Zanmai*, and the *Shodoka* are the oldest Zen texts. In all Zen temples the *Sandokai* and the *Hokyo Zanmai* are always recited together. But as you do not know them, Narita Roshi[7] and I will now chant them for you.

---

[7] Narita Roshi, a disciple of Kodo Sawaki, came from Japan specifically to join Master Deshimaru in Val d'Isere. See Glossary.

Session One: July 27 – July 30, 1977

I will continue the kusen on samsara, transmigration and reincarnation.

To understand profoundly the meaning of samsara, we must rely on nothing but our own deep, subjective feelings. In Buddhism this understanding depends solely upon each separate individual.

In some sutras samsara is refused; in other sutras it is affirmed.

The sutra containing the conversation between the King Milinda of Greece and the Bodhisattva Nagasena goes as follows:

"What is samsara?" asked the King Milinda.

"Oh, great King," replied the Bodhisattva Nagasena, "here we live and die, live and die, live and die. Great King, this is samsara."

"I do not understand. Explain it more deeply."

"Samsara is like a grain of mango," replied the Bodhisattva Nagasena. "We eat the fruit of mango, and still the great mango tree gives more fruit. More fruit is eaten, more seeds are planted, and from these seeds another great mango tree grows and gives more fruit and more seeds. Thus, great King, we live and die, live and die. This is samsara."

In another sutra the Bodhisattva Nagasena denies samsara.

"What does it mean to be born in the next world?" asked the King.

"After death, name, mind and body are not born again," replied Nagasena.

"Then what is our name, mind and body after death?" asked the King.

"Our name, mind and body are not the same. They are karma. And because of this karma, another name, mind and body are born."

Forgetting the ego

Through this sutra we can understand the meaning of the reappearance of life and death. It does not mean a reappearance of name, mind and body. These are merely forms. Only our karma reappears. After death there is nothing left but the movement of karma.

The fundamental cosmic power realizes itself in the repetition of life and death. Yet, although this is so, this power should be realized through our own personal will; it should be realized through mind and body.

There is no substance, no noumenon, in our mind and body. This is the teaching of Buddhist philosophy. That there is no noumenon means that we live by the power of the cosmic order. We move and we evolve through our actions, through our karma—that is, through our vocal expressions, our body, our mind, our consciousness. When we abandon ourselves, when we detach ourselves, when we do not entertain a consciousness in our minds, our body and mind follow the cosmic order. And so we obtain fully the cosmic order. Zazen is the best method for obtaining this cosmic energy.

Master Dogen has said that to study Buddhism means to study the ego. To grasp the ego means to abandon it, to forget it. This is very difficult to do. But through zazen it is possible.

When we are in pain we forget the ego. When we concentrate on our pain, the pain gets worse. So you must concentrate on the position of your fingers, on your posture. Chin in, stretch the backbone.

Manpo is very important—*man* means everything; *po* means all existence, all the cosmos. To be enlightened we must receive certification through the entire cosmos. When we abandon the ego, when we forget it, we become the entire cosmos. Both our body and our mind become it.

Datsuraku[8]—remove, throw away. This is like a metamorphosis of our body and our mind. When this occurs, our body and mind become the entire cosmos. This is zazen.

∽

[Here ends the first sesshin. Those who have attended this camp leave. During the following day, new people arrive, approximately two hundred in number. The Master's closer disciples—here called the "permanents"—remain throughout the entire five weeks.]

---

[8] *Datsu* is to take off, to outgrow itself; *raku* is to throw down. See pp. 138-140.

OPPOSITE: *Mushin*—Non-mind, detachment

Session Two

August 1 – August 9, 1977

Letting go of thoughts

The practice of zazen is the process of becoming intimate with oneself. One does not look outside oneself. During zazen it is necessary to concentrate on your posture, but you must forget about the body. This is a contradiction, a koan. We must look into ourselves, look into our minds. We must observe our minds.

In the *Fukanzazengi* by Master Dogen, it is written that we must think about non-thinking. That is, we must think from the bottom of non-thinking. Do not think about thinking, says Master Dogen. Think non-thinking. How? How do we not-think about thinking? Through Hishiryo.

Hishiryo is absolute thinking. In terms of contemporary physics this means to stop the thinking process which occurs in our frontal brain, and to think, instead, with our body. That is, to stop the thinking process of our personal consciousness. However, if personal thoughts do arise, it is not necessary to stop them. Just observe them, as you would a dream.

In zazen your mind becomes like a mirror. When your subconscious mind arises, it arises as though in a mirror. And so you can observe it objectively. Subjective thoughts which appear in the mind are merely the arising of bad karma and bonnos. So when they appear, let them pass, like in a mirror. A mirror itself is not bad.

Here is a poem called "Zazen" by Master Dogen:

Without muddiness
In the water of the mind,
Clear is the moon.
Even the waves break upon it,
And are changed into light.

Zen is zazen, which is Shikantaza. Shikantaza is the essence of Zen. Even if you were to read a thousand books and Buddhist sutras, without the practice of zazen you would miss it. It would be like painting an apple on paper.

~

Today begins the second camp. After the morning zazen, we strike the *kaijo*.[9] This drum signifies the hour. In the large temples in Japan, such as Eiheiji, they sound the hour with the big bell. Then we strike the *han*[10] with gathering momentum. The han is struck in three series. At the beginning of the third series, the big kaijo is struck by the *Tenzo*[11] in the kitchen. With these sounds terminated, we place our Rakusus on top of our heads, and, with our hands in gassho, we recite the *Kesa Sutra*. Next the Kyosaku-man ends the zazen by hitting the bell with one stroke. Then we turn about, and the ceremony takes place. We chant the *Hannya Shingyo*.

Living without calculating

What is Satori? . . . There is no need to seek Satori. Do zazen; the zazen itself is Satori.

Through your zazen posture you can harmonize with the great nature, with the cosmos. You can be in unity. In modern civilization most people go in the opposite direction to nature. Not just in their daily lives, but in their thinking, too. Most people are always calculating, always running after sex, money and food. And those who do not act this way dwell upon it in their minds. It is in their minds.

What is true love? The love of most people is egoistic. "I help women—I am a Bodhisattva." This is egoistic. A Bodhisattva is someone who has completely abandoned the ego to devote himself to others.

All the phenomena of our life become truth. The *Genjo Koan* by Master Dogen—*genjo* means all phenomena; while *koan*, here, means the truth, the Dharma. To study Buddhism means to

---

[9] *Kaijo*: The drum.
[10] *Han*: The wood.
[11] *Tenzo*: The Chief Cook.

study the ego. To study the ego means to forget the ego. To forget the ego means zazen. With the exact zazen posture, you can forget yourself naturally, unconsciously, automatically.

To forget ego means to be certified by all the cosmos, by all existence. We must understand that when we forget ego, all the cosmos, all existence becomes ego. When we forget ego, all ego returns to the cosmos. When we die, we enter the coffin—and at this moment we can return to the cosmos. Our body and our mind, at this moment, can return to the cosmos. With zazen it is the same: we can return to the cosmos.

[As the Master speaks, someone is being helped out of the Dojo by the Kyosaku-man.]

People who are sick in some way, and especially those with sick nerves, will feel a strong reaction. But never mind. It is the zazen. Zazen is very strong.

∼

All people who practice Soto Zen must first understand the *Fukanzazengi*. When I first met my Master Kodo Sawaki, he gave me a copy of the *Fukanzazengi*. It was very difficult for me to understand this text, written in ancient Japanese.

I will now sing the *Fukanzazengi* with Narita Roshi.

The *Fukanzazengi* was written by Master Dogen while he was at Koshogi Temple in Kyoto. Until this time, women were not allowed to enter Buddhist temples. Dogen, however, opened the Temple of Koshogi to men and women alike, and so women throughout Japan came to Koshogi to practice zazen.

Fukan means to spread zazen among all people. *Zazengi* are the rules of zazen: how we do zazen, how we think during zazen, how we breathe, and how we maintain the correct posture.

Now we will sing.

One kesa, one poem

This morning Narita Roshi and Mr. Fukada[12] will be leaving us. Narita Roshi will be rejoining his disciples in Japan, and Mr. Fukada his Dojo in London. I thank them very much for having joined us in Val d'Isére. I want to thank Narita Roshi especially. He has much work at his temple in Japan, and he has many disciples waiting for him to return, and yet he has spent so much time with us and has taught us many things.

Narita Roshi wishes to offer me, after this morning's zazen, his big Kesa which he is now wearing. This is what he wrote on the envelope of the Kesa: "The absolute essence of the true Kesa. This Kesa, coming from the Todenjo Temple at Akita in Japan, is the true, great Kesa consisting of twenty-five rows,[13] and in the color of mokuran. Given to the Temple by Kodo Sawaki, this Kesa has been transmitted twenty-seven times from Master to Master; and, I, Narita Roshi, am the twenty-eighth. This Kesa is a Temple treasure, and so it has been strenuously protected.

"This Kesa, transmitted to me from Master Kodo Sawaki—here, at this moment, I offer it to you. I transmit it to you, Taisen Deshimaru. This Kesa is the true essence of Zen, the true *Shobogenzo*,[14] the true Dharma. So please promote it; transmit this Zen to all humanity.

"I want to celebrate and dedicate it to you and to your mission, and to all Europe, and to all people. To exalt the Zen of Master Dogen, that it may save all mankind, and for peace in the world. I celebrate deeply, and with respect, this August 2, 1977.

"I am very happy to have done zazen here with you in Val d'Isére."

I will receive this Kesa from Narita Roshi after zazen and before the Buddha.

I wish to present and to offer to Narita Roshi a new Kesa, made and sewn by my disciples Mokutai Seishin (Jeanne) and

---

[12] Mr. Fukada: Head of the London Dojo.
[13] Symbolizing twenty-five furrowed rows in a rice field.
[14] *Shobogenzo*: The treasury-eye of the True Teaching. See Glossary.

Taigyaku Shoren (Anne-Marie). Here is what I wrote on the envelope: "The sound of the valley is a long, great conference. The form, the color of the mountain, is the true body of purification. This mountain is beautiful nature; it is the true body of Buddha. From dusk to dawn it sings 84,000 poems—how can this deep meaning be explained to others?

"On August third 1977, here in Val d'Isére, listening to the sound of the river in the valley, I am very happy to have received this Kesa, and to have been able to do zazen with you this summer. On this day that you leave for Japan, I dedicate to you this Kesa from Shomon Taisen. I dedicate it with one hundred sampais."

For the Dojo in London, I give a Kesa to Mr. Fukada. On the Kesa I wrote: "The voice of the valley is the great teaching of the Buddha."

And last night, after the bell, I wrote this poem:

When I turn my head in the direction of my past life,
Already more than sixty years have gone by.
During these past times good and bad has happened,
And they have been exactly like in a dream.
During this sesshin in the Alps,
The sound of the pure stream in the valley;
At midnight elegant and rapid sounds;
The sound of the stream enters through my empty window.

Looking at one's karma before the final hour

I will continue my kusen on the relationship existing between samsara, reincarnation, transmigration and karma. Today I will give a kusen on the relationship between karma and the cosmos.

Buddha obtained Satori under the Bodhi Tree. He awoke to karma.

Only man, only the human being, can awaken to karma.

In the *Shobo Nenjo Kyo*, an ancient Buddhist sutra, it is written that he who wishes to be born again must, at the moment of his death, imagine the shadowy form of a rock falling upon him.

The rock falls upon him, covering his entire body. The man who wishes to be reborn again then calls others to his aid to help him remove the rock from on top of him. Such a man, suffering his death throes, observes his past life passing before him. Then, directly before dying, the man imagines, dreams, that he is witnessing his father and his mother having sexual intercourse. If such a person wishes to be reborn as a male, he must imagine himself having sexual intercourse with the mother. The father then appears and interrupts them in the act of intercourse. If such a person wishes to be reborn as a female, he must imagine himself having sexual intercourse with the father. The mother appears and interrupts them in the act of intercourse. Directly thereafter the man dies. Life again arises, consciousness reappears, and a new life starts. So it is written in this sutra.

And so begins again the relationship of cause and effect. It is similar to the stamp imprinted in a mold—even if the stamp breaks, its imprint has been made in the mold.

The transmigration factor in this sutra had much influence upon ancient, traditional Hinduism. Buddha, however, accepting only part of this thought on transmigration, modified it and made it more rational. Buddha removed this thought from the after-death concept and used it as an analysis of the living man instead. And so he removed it from the realm of religious mysticism.

Buddha did not use this new attitude on transmigration for any moral purposes. He used it originally as a method for recovering humanity—for healing humanity. And so we have the discovery of personal, individual karma. And since humanity is the source of fundamental cosmic power, personal karma and fundamental cosmic power are connected, related. Buddha's Satori while sitting in zazen under the Bodhi Tree was the objective observation of his karma—of the karma of his entire life.

Getting past attachment

As long as there is attachment, there is no escape from the world of transmigration. Remain in the world of relativity, in the world of good and bad, in the world of morality, and so remain in the world of transmigration. To make gifts, say prayers, carry out good, moral actions (such as did the Indians of ancient times), and obtain good merit, thereby obtaining rebirth in heaven, is but to be reborn into the world of morals.

True Satori is beyond the world of good causes and of good effects, beyond that which makes for good merit and rebirth in heaven, beyond the world of good morals. We must not depend upon the good karma created by our acts—we must not use it. Rather, we must be beyond this world of transmigration, beyond this world of attachment.

Attachment—this is a very important point. Human attachment is instinctive. To be beyond attachment, to cut it, is not a denial of humanity. To deny attachment is to change oneself; it is to change humanity itself. How can we change humanity? Is this possible?

Yesterday's ego is not today's

During zazen we are observing ourselves. We are observing ourselves subjectively—we are observing ourselves objectively. So when I say, "Today I must give someone here the *rensaku*,"[15] everyone wonders if perhaps it is not he himself who is to receive the rensaku. "Maybe it's for me! Last night I wasn't so good. I stole two hundred francs. Not so good. I am a thief." A thief for two hundred francs. Steal one franc and you are a thief. It comes back. Bad karma.

[Apparently someone stole some money.]

However, if the thief reflects profoundly and if he then confesses his theft, his ego will change.

[The Master addresses the thief.]

I will give you two hundred francs if you come to me and confess. No, I will give you a thousand francs. This way you can

---

[15] *Rensaku*: A series of blows given with the kyosaku on the muscles located between the neck and shoulders. Its purpose is to educate, not to punish.

make money. Of course, if you confess simply to make more money if this is your object—then it is not so good. It is not Mushotoku.

Last night I spoke about how one can change humanity. In the sutra dealing with the King Milinda and the Bodhisattva Nagasena, Milinda asked the Bodhisattva: "Is it possible not to be born into the next world?"

"Oh, great King," replied the Bodhisattva, "when a person wishes not to be born into the next world, certainly he can know it."

"How can he know this?" asked the King.

"If a man cuts off the reason, the cause, for his being born into the next world," replied the other, "then he can understand this, he can know this."

So, if we do not dwell upon the reason why we are born into the next world, we are not born into it. Transmigration and reincarnation are not repeated.

Someone, during a mondo in the last sesshin, asked me why it was that we are born into the next world. I replied that if you do not wish to be born, you will not be born. I had thought that the person who had asked me this question was seeking a way to avoid going to Naraka. People who are afraid of their bad karma want to avoid rebirth. On the other hand, people who want to go to heaven, to go to paradise, seek rebirth.

Neither of these attitudes is good. Both are moral positions. One must be beyond such positions. Buddha denied transmigration. On the other hand, he acknowledged it.

If you want to be beyond the world of morals, you must understand why transmigration arises. Why does transmigration arise? This is an important question.

This is zazen. The reason is zazen. Through the practice of zazen, you can come to understand this. This is Satori. Such an understanding does not come about through brainthinking. It must be experienced through the body—religiously.

There is no noumenon. There is no substance. There is no substance of transmigration in the body. What is zazen? It is *muga*. Muga is non-noumenon. And the ego? The ego is always in change. Yesterday the person who stole the money was a thief. This morning, when the thief heard me say that he must receive the rensaku, he was frightened, he realized that he had not done a very good thing, and so his ego changed. Yesterday's ego is not today's. Mind changes. Body too.

The flame of our actions continues
To cut off our attachments is to cut off transmigration. This does not mean that we cut off our lives. Transmigration has no substance, no noumenon. So, as there is no noumenon, there is no necessity to cut off anything. When a person wishes to continue his life, when he wishes not to die, when he wishes that he be reborn, this person is attached to life. This is ego. But if ego has no noumenon, then there is no continuation of life. Without ego-attachment, there need not be transmigration.

Burning wood, like ego, changes all the time. It becomes ashes. Its structure changes. But the flame continues. Karma continues. The flame of karma, the flame of our actions, continues.

Ashes cannot look at the wood; wood cannot look at the ashes. One cannot see his body in ashes; the ashes cannot see oneself. This is because there is no noumenon.

It is not necessary to try and understand this with the brain. We can understand this through zazen.

Shiki soku ze ku, ku soku ze shiki.[16] Ego is *ku*.[17] Ku becomes *shiki*.[18] So here we are, all doing zazen. Now there is no noumenon.

Body and cosmos are not separate
All existence is ku. Existence is merely the different phenomena within this fundamental cosmic power. It is beyond the world of

---

[16] *Shiki soku ze ku*: The subject is in the object. *Ku soku ze shiki*: The object is in the subject. Shiki and Ku are inseparable. The expression is generally translated as Form is emptiness, emptiness is form.
[17] *Ku*: Existence without noumenon.
[18] *Shiki*: Phenomena.

physics and of metaphysics. Beyond materialism, beyond spiritualism. Fundamental cosmic power alone is absolute. Yet, as there is no noumenon to be found within this cosmic force, this cosmic force also is ku.

Ku is not emptiness. Ku has awful and infinite powers. It—this fundamental cosmic power—produces, one by one, all the phenomenal existences in the cosmos; sometimes it also destroys them.

In Christianity it is necessary to have faith in the thought that God is an absolute personal existence. But I think that God also means the fundamental cosmic power itself.

We cannot find any substance in God. We cannot find either, any single, substantial, personal existence anywhere in the cosmos. So God means the invisible, fundamental cosmic power. The fundamental cosmic power cannot vanish, and it cannot finish. So it is with God. God cannot die. God, like the fundamental cosmic power, is absolute eternity.

To believe in the fundamental cosmic power is to have true faith in God. We are each one of us a son of this fundamental power. We are, every one of us, cosmic existence. It is to this that we must awaken ourselves. To be awakened, wrote Master Dogen in the *Genjo Koan*, is to be certified by all existences in the cosmos.

During zazen, as we abandon our ego, we feel, we experience our body unifying itself with the cosmos. Through correct posture, breathing and Hishiryo-consciousness, we can harmonize ourselves with the cosmos. Our ego then enters the cosmos, and, when this occurs, Hishiryo-consciousness becomes the entire cosmos. Our consciousness is then full, and it fills the cosmos.

Our ego enters into and communicates with God, and so it becomes the absolute God itself.

In Tibetan Buddhism, in Tantric Buddhism, and in traditional Hinduism, the symbol for the fundamental cosmic power is called *Shakti*. Shakti, sometimes called the Goddess Maya, can have many meanings. For instance, in Tantric Buddhism it sometimes means the female sexual organ. So when the man's sexual organ enters into the woman's, we have the strong male ego entering into and harmonizing with the cosmos. And when the mutual orgasm occurs, we have Satori. I cannot believe this.

In a higher dimension, this can have a deeper meaning; it can become a symbol of cosmic power and so become a holy matter. But for the general public such a religious doctrine is dangerous.

∼

The ego can become absolute God.

Through zazen you can discover unconsciously, automatically and naturally that the practice of zazen itself is the cosmos.

Shakti means zazen.

And the zazen posture itself is God.

We must have faith in it.

Today I saw someone standing on his head. It is possible to realize the cosmic power upside down, like in Yoga. Or right-side-up, like in zazen. Push the ground with the head, and the cosmos with the feet. Why not? But the problem with Yoga is that one holds on to the cosmos in place of the globe.

Karma, like the ego is without substance
To abandon the ego—during zazen—is to cut off all attachment to the substance of the ego. This is *mushin*. *Mu* means no; *shin* means mind. No-mind. D.T. Suzuki liked to use the term mushin. Master Dogen used the term *Hishiryo*.

The word Hishiryo was first used by Master Sosan in his *Shin Jin Mei*, written in the seventh century. Hishiryo-consciousness is thinking without thinking. Hishiryo cannot be thought. So it is written in the *Shin Jin Mei*.

Muga means no-ego. This means that there is no noumenon to the ego. There is no noumenon to karma either. This means that we can cut off any and all transmigration, any and all reincarnation of our ego.

In the *Vissuddimaggi Sastra*[19] it is written that there is no maker of karma and no receiver of its effects. There is only a multitude of phenomenal existences which are being produced one by one, one after the other. This is the correct opinion. So karma, with its consequent effects (results), becomes in turn the cause. Just as in the relationship between the tree and the seed: if transmigration is not recognized (realized) before the occurrence of the phenomenon, transmigration in a future time will not occur. So it is written in this sutra.

As the substance of transmigration is nonexistent, only the karma of phenomenal existences is produced. Yet through our mistaken imagination we believe that a substance is produced (reborn) from past to present, and from present to future.

Karma means simply the cause of karma and the effect of karma. But this (the cause and the effect) is not fixed, and as it does not have any noumenon, it is therefore without existence.

The cause of karma and the effect of karma are both ku.

So, since there is no cause of karma and no effect of karma, the nothingness of the substance of transmigration means the action of karma and not the action of substance. It does not mean emptiness.

The stopped (or fixed) substance is denied in Buddhist thought; the moving (or action) of karma is affirmed. All movement is simply the action of karma.

As I have already explained, action, in the human world, is the fundamental cosmic power realizing the ego.

So, in Buddhism, transmigration is part of the immortal, indestructible cosmic power awakened through human action. It is the immortality of human acts and of human action.

This is the basic principle of karma.

---

[19] *Sastra*: A commentary on a sutra.

A new humanity

Master Dogen wrote in the *Fukanzazengi* that Hishiryo-consciousness is the secret essence of zazen. During zazen we must think, not-think; hear, not-hear; look, not-look; smell, not-smell. So, as to my kusens, even if you do not hear them, you hear them, and hearing them or not-hearing them will bring you good karma in the future. Even if you do not hear this kusen through your personal consciousness, your zazen is hearing it.

∼

Now I will continue my kusen on the relationship between destiny and the human being.

Buddha discovered a new humanity while sitting under the Bodhi tree. This discovery brought to the history of mankind a new form of humanism. Through the doctrine of cosmic energy, he gave a new turn to traditional Hinduism.

In European philosophy, the salvation of the soul did not represent a revival of the human being. In Europe, true salvation, the revival of man, was in direct opposition to the Church and to the traditional authority of God.

Buddha's humanity was built upon the doctrine of fundamental cosmic power, and so there was no denial of the human being. But in Europe during the Renaissance, God's existence was denied for the sake of man's salvation. God was dead. He was sacrificed for the salvation of humanity. So in Europe there arose a negative opposition, a contradiction between the cosmic power of God and the human being. Civilization declined.

European philosophers write philosophy without first understanding themselves. They do not know themselves deeply. They are always looking objectively, without first looking into themselves. These philosophers are always decorating themselves in front of others—this is the true European karma. Manner and behavior are of course very important, but to decorate oneself in front of others is not necessary. I do not want to criticize

European civilization—Oriental civilization is not so good either—I am not here for that. My mission during these last ten years in Europe has been to create an exchange between these civilizations, not to criticize them.

In the Orient they do not deny the cosmic power in order to obtain or recover its humanity. Rather, they base the human specialty upon this cosmic power. As I have repeatedly explained, it is the karma of each individual action alone which moves the human being. The karma of a certain act exists only in the human being. This is the principle of karma.

The doctrines of destiny, of determinism, of fatalism found in Europe do not have anything to do with the doctrine of karma. I now give the rensaku to Taisen Deshimaru and to my secretary, Anne-Marie. I give it to my secretary so as to educate her. And to myself, in order to be taught too. [A dispute arose between the Master and his secretary, and this was the outcome.]

What is true happiness?
Today we begin this second sesshin. Tomorrow, the day after tomorrow, and through half the third day we will be doing a lot of zazen.

What is the most important problem in our lives? How we live and how we die. From the beginning of time, man has asked himself this question of how he should live and how he should die.

What is true happiness? Spiritual and body happiness are both necessary. The body needs food—and sex, too. Over this issue of love and sex many people suffer. And so their karma becomes complicated. During zazen this karma will surface, it will come out of the subconscious, and so you will be able to observe it calmly. And surely, if you continue zazen, you will be able to solve it too—this passion over love and sex.

OPPOSITE: *Shin jin datsu raku*—Fall off, cast off mind and body, which means zazen itself, which means Satori.

身心脱落

How do we eat? During a sesshin we have a special method for eating, and new people are always surprised by it. We use only one bowl, and in the morning it is a bowl of guenmai soup. And before eating we recite a long sutra. Why?

A strong life includes how we eat and how we have sex. During this sesshin we should not look for a woman. It is better that we do not make love. As for food, we should eat simply, mostly vegetables. Once the sesshin is over, you will find a fresh and deep taste for food—and for sex, too.

Through zazen you can find true spiritual happiness. Forget the body, and the mind will become completely solitary.

How do we live eternally? One day we will all be dead and in our coffins. This is so for everyone. And this is why, during my kusens, I talk to you about karma, reincarnation, transmigration or samsara.

By truly observing our interior minds, as can only be done in the zazen posture, we can find true wisdom. Occidentals only observe objectively by looking outside of themselves. Even those here who have continued zazen for some time cannot understand. They do not understand the Master. *I Shin Den Shin* (from Mind to Mind) is very difficult.

There is no one here to whom I can give the Shiho. All here is like theater. Or like the play last night in which one of you played the Master. It was a very good performance. He made a very clever outside picture, but he does not understand the inside of a Master. We have some very intelligent people here who do zazen. But what do they really understand of the Shiho? Of mushin? Of Mushotoku?

Here now in Val d'Isére we are doing zazen along with the sound of the river which flows below the Dojo. We look at the mountains, at the valley, we go on walks. All this is very good certainly. And then at home we have a fast car, we are building a pretty house, and we make love with a beautiful woman—and this is the happiness in our lives. But our lives are not so very long.

How can we influence others? What influence can we have on history? On our civilization?

Session Two: August 1 – August 9, 1977

If you practice zazen, you will find true happiness in your mind. Zazen means to observe all the world, all the cosmos, in your minds. If you practice zazen, it will influence all the cosmos, all the world, all of France, of Switzerland, Germany, the entire Continent, for all time, for eternity.

Karma is not fatalism
During zazen you must stretch the backbone as much as possible, and you must concentrate on your breathing. Concentrate under the belly button, on the *kikai-tanden*. The exhalation of air should be long, and so the inhalation of air will be short and will occur unconsciously and without effort. Thus the body will obtain the *Ki*[20] of cosmic energy. The zazen posture is the best method for obtaining good health, but it is not for that—it is not a method for curing sicknesses. Yet if you practice zazen, you will obtain infinite merit for the body and for the mind.

∼

[The bell for kinhin has been struck and everyone doing zazen stands up.]
In kinhin the breathing is the same as in zazen. With one foot forward, you exhale deeply, and so your knee stretches itself automatically and unconsciously. Kinhin is the best automassage.
[The bell for zazen has been struck and everyone returns to his place.]

∼

Now I will continue my kusen on destiny and karma.
Destiny and karma are not the same. Destiny, in Europe, implies abandonment. It means that God directs (controls) man.

---
[20] *Ki*: Source of life. Body activity. See Glossary.

In Greek mythology there is the Goddess Moira. Every living person, according to this mythology, is a part of the Goddess Moira. Moira, therefore, means the goddess of destiny. And so one's personal assortment is beyond the reach of one's own will. Since one's destiny is in the hands of God, each individual life is heteronomically determined. The ancient Greek writer Homer has said that if destiny visits you, it matters not how clever or brave you are, you will not be able to escape the hand of destiny.

This concept eventually developed into what is known as fatalism—God's will governs all. So how to become free from this fatalistic and deterministic attitude is an important question here in the West. In European philosophical, psychological and theological doctrines, these questions are dealt with, but still these thinkers have not been able to explain how one can escape from the concepts of destiny and fatality. Because they do not go into the problem deeply enough, they have no method for dealing with it. How does one escape from one's miserable destiny? From one's bad karma? They have no real answers to these questions. They have no method, even, for understanding themselves.

Ancient Greek and Indian civilizations were influenced by one another. And sometimes their mythologies were even identical. In ancient Indian thought, Shakti, which means—among other things—fundamental cosmic power, held to three principles or concepts: that of creation, that of preservation, and that of destruction. Likewise, in Greek mythology, the three goddesses Klothe, Lachesis and Athopos represent in turn the goddess who oversees man in birth, the goddess who oversees man in life, and the goddess who presides over man in death. Athopos is the goddess who, in the end, cuts off life.

The gods, in the Occidental world, have always directed the lives of men—from their births, through their daily lives, right through to their deaths. This concept is somewhat similar to that of ancient India in which the God Brahma directs creation, Vishnu protection, and Shiva destruction.

But the doctrine of fatalism in Greek mythology and that of karma in India are not the same. In ancient Greece, birth, life and death were under the direct control of the three goddesses. In India, creation, protection and destruction are under the control of the absolute power of Shakti, or the fundamental cosmic power.

According to the doctrine of karma, we can obtain true freedom through our own personal effort, through human will. This is karma. Sometimes we find ourselves following the cosmic current, at other times not. This too is karma.

Karma is directed by the fundamental cosmic power. Nonetheless, we can go beyond its limits, beyond our own limitations, and so change our karma. We are free to become truly free.

In modern times Herman Hesse, the writer, said that our destiny exists inside ourselves, not outside. Talking more subjectively, he dealt with the fatalistic doctrine by saying that destiny develops in our own minds. Hesse was influenced by Buddhism.

~

Some people here are sleeping. It is necessary to give those who sleep the kyosaku.

If you listen to my kusen or if you do not listen, if you hear it or if you do not hear it, it will not disturb your zazen. It is necessary, during zazen, that your body and your mind be stimulated by a great teaching. When the body is tired, the mind will become sleepy. The body hears my kusens, and so my kusens will become part of your deep-seated memory. This is profound karma for the brain.

During zazen you can obtain Satori even by the sound of the river.

Becoming truly free

When my disciple Michel informed me that he had found an establishment in Val d'Isére, he said: "It is in a valley surrounded by mountains, *Sensei*.[21] It is a fine place, but the sound of the river by the Dojo is very loud and it might disturb our zazen practice." But I thought not. And now that we are here, I thought to myself that I would like to explain to Narita Roshi about the sound of the river. So I wrote him a poem about how the river has already given us 84,000 sutra-poems. The sound of the river is giving us a great conference, going on from morning to midnight.

For some of you the sound of the river is just noise. You try to get beyond it, to escape it, or to conquer it. That is very difficult to do. It is better to become intimate with the sound than to try and conquer it. Then you will become profound.

Nietzsche has written that to conquer one's destiny is difficult, while to be indifferent to it is not so good. He felt that one should become intimate with one's destiny, that one should love it. But Nietzsche was a determinist. Our destiny is not necessarily determined. Nietzsche never really analyzed profoundly this question of destiny.

Other Europeans too, such as Leibniz, dealt with the question of finding harmony in our destiny; and Spengler and Keyserling dealt with the destiny of European civilization on the whole. But they too never really went deeply into the problem. That people should accept their destiny is very fine—but what about those who suffer because of this destiny of theirs? It is not so easy for them to simply accept it, to love it.

The question is: Who is it or what is it which determines our destiny? And how can we analyze this destiny of ours? Through an understanding of karma you can analyze profoundly this question of destiny.

I always say the same thing: to practice zazen is to become intimate with one's ego. My Master Kodo Sawaki also said this.

---

[21] *Sensei*: Japanese for Teacher.

Session Two: August 1 – August 9, 1977

Master Dogen, using another expression, said that Buddhism means to forget the ego. For him zazen was to forget the ego. There are many other expressions. For instance, zazen can also mean to understand the ego, or to conquer it, or to be beyond it. All these are true.

Through zazen we can resolve our destiny—and our karma too. The questions of solitude, of the ego, and of sex too can be resolved. You must become intimate with sex—but this is not so good. This is a koan. Abandon sex, conquer it, understand it, go beyond it. Forget, abandon, conquer, understand, go beyond solitude, too. And so with karma. How can we understand our karma? How do we observe it? How can we cut it off? How can we conquer it? How can we go beyond it?

To reflect properly upon this question of destiny, we must have a vision empty of the illusions created by man.

No one can create your destiny for you.

Karma itself teaches us that we have our own personal illusions about destiny. This too is karma.

So karma includes destiny. Nonetheless, if we observe carefully our karma, we can cut off the illusions. And in so doing, we can then jump into a higher dimension—into a dimension of true freedom.

This desire for true freedom, for true freedom of action and true freedom of behavior, is but the other side of karma. It has nothing to do with modern behaviorism. Anyway, this action is the principle of karma.

The doctrine of fatalism is inbred with the hope for eternity. In its fundament, fatalism is an act of surrendering. We surrender to fatalism, and so we hope for eternity. So we create the term (word) destiny, and so we also create the vision of destiny.

But karma is not vision, nor is it illusion. Rather it is intuition over the eternal power of nature. But karma is also reality which enters into intuition.

∼

Everybody here is sleeping. The kyosaku is necessary. During zazen the kyosaku is very effective, but sometimes it makes too much noise and so it disturbs your zazen. It is very difficult to become intimate with the whack of the kyosaku because it scares people. So now I am having it given all at once. There are now four Kyosaku-men walking behind you.

Someone is crying. A woman. Women often have no patience. You must not disturb the others; if you do you must leave the Dojo. But it is good to cry. That way the bad karma arises from the subconscious and goes out.

∼

Do not become an object of the five sense organs. Reality of mind, reality of thought, reality of intuition are not objects of the five sense organs. But this does not mean that they are not real.

The truth is beyond the five sense organs. We can understand this through the practice of zazen.

The real truth cannot be explained through the mouth. This is why I always say: *I Shin Den Shin* (from Mind to Mind). The pure wind, the clear moon cannot be painted, not even abstractly.

Anyway, to conclude this kusen: the doctrine of karma includes fatalism, and at the same time it is beyond it. Karma is intuition, and through a deep understanding of karma man can find true freedom.

Nothing other than existence
Now I will talk about karma and European causality.

The law of causality establishes the relationship between cause and effect. People, in using their good sense, in using their minds rationally, believe that there is a relationship between cause and effect, and this is how they understand karma. This is an error. Karma and causality are not the same thing. One's life is not directed merely by causality—causality is the relationship between one single cause and its effect.

Session Two: August 1 – August 9, 1977

In European philosophy, causality and rationality are equated. However if we look deeply into this question, we see that causality is not at all rational, but rather it is nonrational. True rationality is reality. Yet that which is reasonable is not necessarily rational. In fact, rationality is not reality—as, for instance, in the case of metaphysics, philosophy and religion.

Generally speaking, reality is what makes up our daily lives. If we separated ourselves from daily living, our lives would have no meaning.

Our lives are complicated; they are composites. And so true religion must grasp our lives in their totality—in all their composites. The object of philosophy is also to grasp this totality, but it cannot. We cannot find, in the world of philosophy, even one side which is certain. It is the same with psychology. Psychology can tell us of the internal mind, certainly, but it cannot create. It cannot create a new, fresh and living activity, for it looks at people objectively, not subjectively. And this is why there is no creativity in psychology. Even were it capable of explaining the different and varying aspects of bonnos, it could never bring about the state of Satori. In brief, psychology cannot change man's vision of life.

People interpret religion in many different ways. Some consider it a philosophy, or a form of psychology, or an art; others see it as a means to obtaining good health.

Religion, in fact, is a composite of human nature. And so religion alone can grasp the totality of life.

Karma, causality... and beyond

Causality is the relationship between a single cause and its effect. This is not so with karma; karma is the relationship between many, many causes and their effects, and this is indelibly tied in with the doctrine of interdependence. Western philosophers, theologians and intellectuals are always mistaken on this account. And because of their false notions on this subject, there have arisen many mistaken interpretations of Buddhism and of karma.

There is not only cause in karma, but interdependence too, and so we have many effects arising. As there is no unique cause, there is no unique result. A man's life is more complex than that.

Certainly with our will we can direct and control our lives. But this is difficult, and sometimes we cannot direct our lives through sheer will, regardless of how strong our will might be. As, for instance, with drugs, or sex, or masturbation, or whiskey—these things are not so easy to stop by sheer willpower. And then there may be all sorts of reasons which make stopping even more difficult: "My wife drinks, and as I am compassionate, I drink with her. She says that she will divorce me if I don't." So there are many causes which contribute to making up our karma.

The social environment in which we live has a big influence on our lives, and so on our karma. But with this sesshin we can become purified. Most people cannot understand this element of cause in karma. They are ignorant. In Sanskrit this state of ignorance is called *Avidya*. However, if we do zazen, wisdom will arise unconsciously, automatically and naturally.

[After kinhin, when all were returning to their places, the Master said:] You must go faster; we are no longer doing kinhin. There is a prize for the last person to sit down. It goes to my disciple Stephane.

∼

In 1969 I received a bad shock. My secretary Madame Rose-Marie was killed in a car accident in a Paris suburb, on a snow-covered road. In the newspapers it was written that the accident was caused by a collision with a cement truck. The next day the police said the accident was caused by a loose wheel—the front left wheel was found a good distance from the accident. Then a doctor who examined the body found that she had just finished eating and that her stomach was full of food. She was tired from the night before, and so sleepiness added to a full stomach could very well have been the cause. And then there is also the question of poor judgment. In any case, even in a car accident the causes are multiple. There is never one simple cause.

It is the same with someone who murders another. The police look for many causes, but in the end the person goes to prison anyhow. And once in prison, the man is interviewed by his lawyer and by the psychologist, and yet they cannot really understand, either, the deep interior mind of the prisoner. For the mind is always in change.

It is subjective religious reflection which in the final analysis is the most significant, the most important. Science, with its reasoning and its objective analysis of the causes in question, is insufficient, so we must find a true relationship between science and religion.

Ten thousand causes, ten thousand effects

If you are simplistic, lack intelligence, or are just plain ignorant, you cannot become happy. "I am considerate with others, I give what I can, and I always try to make an effort in the right direction, and on top of that I practice zazen and have done so for a long time, and yet I am not happy. I do not understand why this is so." This is because there is not just one cause, but numerous causes, which bring about not one effect, but numerous effects.

And so it is with science and medicine. Today there are many different sorts of medicines on the market. But if we abuse the use of such medicines—if we take too many pills of one sort, for instance—our bodies will undergo a reaction to them, and another sickness will arise. Maybe cancer. Many doctors, treating the body as a simplistic mechanism, base their diagnosis on the principle of one cause and one effect. They ignore the principle of interdependence. And so they overlook the obvious: that, for instance, nervousness directly affects the stomach and the brain; or that a poor liver is often related to an angry temperament; or that a troubled gallbladder makes for physical weakness; or that bad kidneys will have a negative influence on the heart and, vice versa, a bad heart will influence the kidneys. Those who eat too much have poor circulation of the blood; they have gas and poison in their systems, and their bodies stink. And with a poisoned stomach, the intestines will not function properly—so stomach and intestines, which are interdependent with the brain, are a major area of sickness in modern times. In a word, all our internal organs are interrelated, and if one of them becomes sick, eventually they will all become so.

During zazen, it is not only your mind which you come to understand, but your body too. For instance, if your stomach or your lungs are in poor condition, you will know this because you will feel it. When we fall sick, it is our weak points which are affected first.

Our existence cannot be seen in isolation

Science today does not disavow interdependence, but it puts little importance on it. And so, still today, one sort of medicine is prescribed for one sort of illness. But in the future the importance of interdependence will become more apparent, and when this occurs, scientists will begin to observe the totality of the body before making their diagnosis.

But one must have wisdom to see the totality. In zazen one observes the totality of both body and mind.

In European philosophy the approach is always progressive. From cause to effect, cause to effect. In an ever-increasing pattern. First the cause, then the effect. The pattern is based in time, and not on a mutual relationship. For Westerners cause and effect cannot happen simultaneously, let alone effect occur before cause. This is how they think.

But this is not how life works. Effect can come before cause, for life is not always progressive—it can also be regressive. Of course, if you are dead you cannot progress, nor can you regress. And yet here you are alive, and yet you are like dead, and so you must experience awakening. You must understand that all relationships are mutual, interdependent. Then you will be able to solve all the problems in your daily lives—even those which exist between couples, between man and woman.

Session Two: August 1 – August 9, 1977

The principles of interdependence and of karma show that your lives do not exist by themselves. Nor in zazen do we exist by ourselves. We are directed by an outside force, by a force which is heteronomical. We do not live by ourselves, but by the fundamental cosmic power. It is this which directs us. During zazen we can experience this feeling. And when we do, it is Satori. If you experience this from the bottom of your body and from the bottom of your mind, you will have a great Satori.

Our lives exist in a mutual relationship between the ego and all the other existences in the cosmos. But those who have too strong an ego cannot understand this. They are egoistic, and so they fall sick, and they never become well and they never become happy.

To abandon one's ego is to realize the relationship, the connection which exists with others; to abandon the ego is to obtain the great power which comes from interdependence.

When cancerous cells in the body come into contact with noncancerous cells, these cancerous cells, which are ego cells, kill the noncancerous ones; being strong with ego, they soon conquer the entire body. And so it is, also, with our civilization today. The egoists are the strong ones today. It is this which has precipitated the great crisis in modern civilization.

Those who continue to practice zazen here during this sesshin will lose their egoism. But they must be patient. Then, in the end, even their zazen itself will become Mushotoku—unconsciously, naturally and automatically.

Even the biggest egoist will calm down. But right now there is a woman sitting not far from me who is always pushing, pushing, in order to get closer to me. She pushes those who are sitting between her and me; she pushes Philippe, who in turn pushes my secretary Anne-Marie, who then pushes me. I am sitting by the door, and if the woman pushes anymore, she will push me right out the door.

One single egoistic person influences the others through interdependence. But during a sesshin most of us get over our egos, and when this happens we begin to receive the energy of the cosmos, and through our zazen postures our insides become calm. And so energy arises not only from within our own selves, but from within everyone, from within all existences. This is mutual existence; this is mutual influence; this is what is called Ki.

One branch burning in a fireplace does not create such heat, and such a big flame, as do many branches. If during this three-day sesshin you concentrate profoundly on your zazen, you will feel this in both your body and your mind. This is the principle of interdependence.

Interdependence, a two-way road

It is difficult to explain the principles of interdependence and karma with only words, and even more difficult to explain them through the doctrine of causality.

Innen,[22] which means relationship, occurs when there is interdependence. So Innen is not simply a cause. As explained in the *Vissuddimaggi Sastra*, when En appears, something else appears. When En does not appear, nothing else appears. When En vanishes, the other vanishes.

Our lives, right down to the interaction of bacteria in our bodies, consist of mutual relationships. If certain bacteria are missing in the intestines, the intestines will not function. One can find many examples depicting this—and not just among *sentient beings*,[23] but also among animals and plants, between whom mutual relationships also exist. The question of life and death is of utmost importance to mankind, and in Buddhism this question is dealt with by the logic of interdependence. *Ku soku ze shiki, shiki soku ze ku.* Ku, which is nothing, becomes,

---

[22] *In* is cause; *En* is karma or interdependence. In is the inner and direct cause by which the result occurs; En is the external and indirect one. En is a contributory cause, as distinct from a direct cause. All action occurs in harmony with both In and En.

[23] *Sentient beings*: Individuals who conceive of themselves as being caught up in the endless cycle of birth and death. See Glossary.

through interdependence, something. Shiki, which is phenomena, becomes, through interdependence, ku.

Interdependence, in Sanskrit, is *Pratyaya*, which means to face forward, to go forward. Pratyaya can also mean to come back; to rebound, to jump back. The Sanskrit word Pratyaya can be understood through the image of a ball being thrown against a wall and bouncing back. So it is with a cause: the cause arises, goes, returns. Interdependence is the force of propulsion of the cause. It is the force which causes the effect. And so it is a condition. And so our bodies are, in fact, directed by causality. But through willpower, the mind can affect causality, and so we have the principle of mutual interdependence.

The body is complicated. It has lots of karma—sometimes too much. Therefore, to cut old habits of daily life, of the family, of business and so on, is not easy. But if we practice zazen, we can cut everything; we can then forget the body, and once in this solitary state, we can look objectively into our minds, and so we can become profoundly intimate with ourselves.

Our consciousness can communicate with the cosmos.

To obtain this sort of communication with our bodies is very difficult; but our consciousness is a free and creative force, and so with our consciousness we can communicate with this fundamental power—especially during zazen. At the moment when this is happening, there exists an interdependence with the cosmos. This state of consciousness is not body consciousness. It is Ki—our Ki, our energy, our mind-consciousness in communication with the cosmos. It is true Mind. It is Hishiryo-consciousness. All existences, all phenomena of the world, of the cosmos, so arise and so are produced. This is interdependence.

Human beings cannot be beyond the stream of time, and so they die. Death visits everybody at least once. All Westerners know this. Death exists in time, and so we have the principle of causality (earlier I had said fatalism). The human is ruled, and is thought of, in terms of the time-dimension. But since the doctrines of karma and of interdependence state that we are limited by space and not by time, personal willpower, liberty and happiness can become the directing influences in our lives. This liberty, this freedom, is, however, limited by space. Freedom beyond time and space is a mystical experience. To understand that, in the social world freedom of the will is utterly limited by space is to understand, to awaken to, our karma, our interdependence.

∽

I will continue later for those who are now sleeping. And I will give a mondo, too, for the sleepers.

If, during zazen, you listen to complicated philosophy, that can be a good thing. But if you don't listen, if you don't want to listen, it is as you like; then just concentrate on your zazen posture. It is the same thing. What is best is to listen/not-listen unconsciously, automatically, naturally.

∽

We will now have a mondo A mondo is not at all like questions and answers given in universities. Sometimes a mondo answer is a koan. And sometimes the answer is no answer—particularly when I do not understand the question asked.

MONDO

QUESTION: Sensei, how would you explain the difference between certified Rinzai and certified Soto Satori?
MASTER: In Soto Zen there is no certification of Satori. This is not so in Rinzai Zen. However, the Shiho in Soto does imply certification. In Rinzai they test you with a series of koans; it is like an examination. In Rinzai, Satori is sometimes a special phenomenon. Also, Rinzai disciples develop a particular consciousness from working over these koans, and sometimes there is great tiredness and even madness. Anyway, it is from this particular consciousness that Rinzai Satori arises. This is not the case with Soto Satori.

QUESTION: Can you obtain Satori without practicing zazen?
MASTER: Zazen itself is Satori. You haven't been listening to my kusens. With no zazen, no Satori. Just madness. Zazen is Shikantaza, is Satori.

QUESTION: Sensei, what is Nirvana?
MASTER: Nirvana is entering the coffin.

QUESTION: When we suffer in zazen, is this Satori?
MASTER: Yes. The worse the pain, the more you forget, so you have a big Satori. It is not necessary to think: "Now I am in pain, so I lose my Satori." Satori is not important. When you do not think of Satori, you have Satori.

QUESTION: We must not kill flowers, so then why do we practice *Ikebana*?[24]

---

[24] *Ikebana*: Japanese flower arrangement.

ZEN & KARMA

> MASTER: Don't do Ikebana then. Religion is subjective, so don't worry about others and what they do. In Hinayana Buddhism, which is very different from Mahayana, you cannot even give the Buddha statue a flower.
>
> But to save many people, it is all right to kill one person. So it is written in a sutra. But here, in this case, to choose, to distinguish, this is what is difficult. Once I asked my Master, Kodo Sawaki, why he drank liquor in his room on the Temple grounds. "Over the front gate to the temple," I said to him, "it is written that no liquor is to be brought in through this gate."
>
> "I don't bring it in through the front gate," Kodo Sawaki replied. "I bring it in through the back."

The living nirvana

Death will surely come, for death exists within the stream of time and time is directed by the law of cause and effect.

Fatalism is but one category within this time-limited dimension.

Anyway, to conclude what I said this morning, the soul is infinity. The soul is but karma unending, and the ego is the realization of the fundamental cosmic power. Ego is one among all existences. Ego is part of the cosmic power. We must wake up to this.

Now, today, I will explain the principle of living Nirvana.

When my disciple Stephane asked me in a mondo what Nirvana was, I felt that he had not thought deeply on the subject, and so I simply replied that Nirvana was entering the coffin.

Nirvana, in Sanskrit, means complete death. So why do I speak of living Nirvana? Living Nirvana is the essence of Mahayana Buddhism. It is the essence of zazen. Nirvana is death,

OPPOSITE: *Shi zen* (or *Ji nen*)—Nature; natural, automatic

見花

and yet, in zazen, one must be completely awake, not asleep. This is a contradiction.

Existence seeks eternal life, but it is existence of the mind and not of the body which seeks this. When the body dies, the four elements which make up the body are reabsorbed into the cosmos. And so the elements of the body are unending. Likewise, since mind and body are in unity, the mind, like the body, remains eternally in the cosmos. Therefore, if it is our wish, our desire, to live in eternity, it is possible to do so—for eternity exists. And the desire for it is the realization of it. This is called living Nirvana, and though this state is not referred to as the here-and-now, it can be obtained here and now. It is, in fact, zazen. This is the great hope of man: to live on—if not in body, then in mind.

Mistaken methods

One sort of method used in order to obtain eternal mind is the practice of asceticism. Asceticism is based on the practice of cutting off all the bonnos of the body. By cutting off all the obstacles caused by the body, one's mind can live on and on, like a shining light.

Alexis, don't move! Otherwise we will give you the kyosaku . . . Oh, he does not understand. He is only five.

Now there is another method used for obtaining living Nirvana, and this method is the exact opposite of the one just described. The first method, which requires great patience, is based on the technique of crushing the bonnos within the body, of pushing them within. The other method is based on burning up the poisons, the bonnos, of the body—on in fact pushing them out and not in. The approach here is to take such bonnos as overeating, sex, love and so on, and practice them unto exhaustion—this results in a state of fatigue in which we no longer have the desire to overeat, to practice sex, to fall in love. And with these bonnos—such as sex, for instance—once and for all erupted, our desires become utterly quiet, and our minds tranquil and without trace of lingering bonnos. So it is with Tantric Buddhism.

Great religious doctors use one or the other of these methods, the one being based on patience, the other being equivalent to masturbation. The one absorbs its poisons from within; the other rids them from without.

However, we must not forget that the object in all this is to reach the state of living Nirvana, and so both these methods are but means to a higher dimension. But in so doing, one must not indulge oneself in the method itself—that is, one must not get lost in this task of ridding ourselves of the bonnos of the body. For otherwise we will never come into communication with the fundamental cosmic power.

Neither of these two methods is sufficiently exact; they are lacking in perfection and they are not complete enough for one who wishes to attain to the fundamental cosmic power.

Shakyamuni Buddha himself experienced both these methods. Buddha, living in the palace and surrounded by the loveliest women and furnished with the best of food, indulged himself to saturation. So he escaped from this life, from this "method," and following the traditional Hindu meditation and Yoga methods of the times, he practiced asceticism for six years—until he was almost dead from lack of food and from exhaustion. After experiencing these two methods, he finally came to practice zazen. And, in so doing, he attained the great Satori when he saw the morning star from his seat under the Bodhi Tree. Nagarjuna[25] too experienced both these methods, and so did Bodhidharma. But after his arrival in China and his encounter with the Emperor, Bodhidharma concentrated solely on Shikantaza—on zazen. Of course he did *pipi*, and he slept too, and he even practiced karate. But he concentrated on only one thing: zazen.

All the great Masters of the Transmission, in fact, experienced these two methods.

---

[25] *Nagarjuna*: (100–200) Famous Indian Buddhist philosopher and Fourteenth Patriarch in the line from the Buddha. He was the founder of the Madhyamika (or Middle Way) School of Buddhism. See Glossary.

To cut off our bonnos through asceticism is, indeed, very difficult to do. And, contrarily, to attempt to attain the higher dimensions through the practice of sexual Tantrism is plain dangerous—particularly for the normal, general public. Mistakes happen easily, and then bad karma is created. And what is more, because it is open to criticism and attack by the world of moralists, who fear for their moral codes, sexual Tantrism is inevitably influenced by these outside attacks.

I wish to say by this that zazen (which, in itself, includes these two methods) is the only balanced method for attaining the absolute and utterly complete living Nirvana here and now and directly, for zazen is beyond asceticism and Tantrism.

What always endures
We cannot deny the eternal existence of the material body, nor that of the spiritual mind. Contrarily, at our death we cannot affirm eternal existence either. Likewise, even at our death we cannot affirm that though the body dies, the soul lives on. But as we can affirm—for it is a fact—that after death the elements of our body remain in the cosmos, so we can affirm that our mind also remains in the cosmos. Therefore we can say that this mind, which has not to do with an entity, with a soul, is but the karma of this mind.

I would also like to make another important point: that this karma of our body and mind, this ego of our body and mind, has no substance, no noumenon. Our karma, our ego, is directed by the fundamental cosmic power—by virtue of its interdependence with all existences. Substance does not exist after death; our karma, though, in terms of phenomena, does exist—and so, because of its interdependence with all existences, our karma continues into eternity. Our karma, seen as phenomena, is referred to in German as *das wahrhaft seiende*. It is the stream of existence, the stream of ourselves within the great cosmic order.

So, if it is our wish, our desire, our hope, to live on into the long eternity, then so be it. Our mind can live on in the eternity of the cosmos.

This is the highest happiness man can find. This is living Nirvana.

~

Concentrate. The last moments in zazen are the most fruitful. If you are passing through big difficulties now, your zazen can solve them, for zazen itself is living Nirvana. Some here are not in happiness; their zazen is too painful. They do not need, do not want, living Nirvana. But if they continue in their concentration, they will understand.

> **MONDO**
>
> QUESTION: Sensei, since certification of Satori is considered so important in Zen Buddhism, how was Shakyamuni Buddha's Satori certified?
> MASTER: By the fundamental cosmic power. By the morning star. Shakyamuni Buddha never said that he had obtained Satori. He completely understood by his body and his mind, and he became unity. He forgot everything at that time, and he felt his body and his mind in harmony with cosmic power—by experience. You, each of you, must experience this yourselves.
>
> QUESTION: You talk about Ki. Is Ki a form of breathing too?
> MASTER: Ki is concentration on only one time, one moment. *Kiai*[26]! That is Ki. In one moment kill the other. Sometimes I use this method when I chant the *Kito Sutra*[27]: Kiai! It is not mystical or magic power.

---

[26] *Kiai*: A shout used primarily in the martial arts. It is an expression of the Ki—the process of activity becoming voice, of activity arising through voice.
[27] *Kito Sutra*: See Glossary.

QUESTION: Are your kusens really necessary during zazen?

MASTER: It is not necessary to listen to my kusens. It is the same as the torrent in the valley. But without kusens you think of your illusions: "What do we eat today?" "Oh, I want to enter mademoiselle's room." "How can I escape from here?" So I say: "Don't move! Chin in!" This is a big kusen. Understand?

REPLY: No.

MASTER: If you don't want to hear my kusens you must go out. It would be better for you to do zazen outside the Dojo. For beginners sometimes it is better outside. Understand?

REPLY: No.

MASTER: You have too much ego. You do zazen outside.

QUESTION: What is *Kensho*?

MASTER: It means looking at your true nature. A technical Rinzai word, Kensho. Rinzai people always want discussion. Kensho is looking at one's Satori.

In Soto, the true Master wants others to look so that others can certify it. This is why Rinzai Kensho is a forbidden teaching in Soto Zen.

If we look into ourselves, we see only that we have no noumenon. This is what the Buddha saw. Only this. He saw that he was without substance; he saw that his noumenon was the fundamental cosmic power—that he himself was the fundamental cosmic power.

It is only *after* the Buddha saw this that men came to say that the Buddha had Satori. The Buddha never said it.

Kensho is not necessary. We all know we have no noumenon. Buddha taught this. Zazen is more important.

The soul

Zazen attains living Nirvana. It is no-mind. It is Hishiryo. It is absolute thinking. It is beyond thinking. It is abandoning the ego. It is forgetting the ego. It is forgetting the ego within the fundamental cosmic power. And so it is certified philosophically, and so it is certified by the cosmic power. Living Nirvana is profound religious communication with the cosmic force.

Tantric Buddhists believe that, after experiencing complete sexual satisfaction, they are in empty-mind, and so they can attain living Nirvana. Ascetics believe that, with the body dead, the mind awakens, and so they too attain living Nirvana. The one attains empty-mind through sexual satisfaction; the other through cutting it off altogether.

Though these two methods are opposed to each other, they both have the same object—to cut off the bonnos.

These methods are not natural. It is not necessary to cut off the bonnos. Zazen is beyond this—it is beyond Tantric Buddhism and beyond asceticism.

To live eternally is the highest happiness for man. That his soul be immortal, this is his wish. And so, since ancient times, saints, wise men and religious people have thought about this. But no matter what they have thought, they too have died. Their names have become famous, their teachings, their holy words, their minds still exist—and so too their tombs. But not their souls. People are saddened by the death of a body. I experienced this myself in childhood with the death of my grandmother. I shook her coffin and said, "Why are you dead?" She had always liked me, but this didn't change anything—she stayed dead. Then they placed her body on the funeral pyre, and I watched it burn. This was in the provinces, where you could still attend such occasions. And so I watched the red flame and the blue smoke, and the body completely lost in smoke, and the strong stink. All this made everybody sad.

Even though her body was burning up, her soul, at least, still existed—or so I hoped. I did not want her soul to burn up, too. Then, years later, when I came to Paris, I received another shock when my secretary Rose-Marie died in a car accident. They put her body in a coffin and buried it, and again I became very sad. Again I hoped that her soul would remain in this world. But this thought is an aspect of egoism. Egoism causes us to be anxious about what occurs after death.

In Buddhism, this question of the immortality of the soul is not discussed. This is not for sentimental reasons, but because the question cannot be resolved through discussion or through reason, for it is a question of intuition.

Since ancient times people have wanted to believe in the immortality of the soul. And regardless of what has been said to the contrary, religious and spiritual people do not deny it—for they too wish to believe in eternity, in the pure spirit.

Kant has said that this belief in the immortality of the soul stems from a fundamental human need, like a prerequisite. But I think not. I think it is, rather, a cherished human desire.

People wish for the soul to live on in eternity, and also they wish for the body itself to go on as long as possible. So it is in Catholicism, too. Their bodies are buried in a cemetery, maybe to go into the sky. In modern times in America, as the Americans here well know, there is special care taken of dead bodies, and in the American funeral parlors they even try to make the dead bodies look alive. What they want is for the dead body to live eternally. Clearly we must resolve this problem for ourselves, once and for all.

Buddha negated the immortality of body and soul. He wanted bodies to be burned to prevent attachment. In Buddhism we burn the body. No attachment.

In the sutra dealing with the Greek King Milinda and the Bodhisattva Nagasena, there is a discussion on this question of the existence of a soul, and on the existence of a noumenon. The Sanskrit word *Vedago* means soul. Anyway, the King asked the Bodhisattva: "Does a soul exist or not?"

The Bodhisattva replied: "It does not exist."

(In ancient times people thought that the blue smoke or flame sometimes seen in a cemetery after it has rained, or on the funeral pyre on which the body is burning, was the soul itself. So this question of the King's was based specifically on the reality of the soul. Of course, in modern times everyone knows that this blue flame is but a chemical phosphorescent.)

Afterwards the King's questions took on a higher dimension; they became more philosophic. He asked Nagasena: "Does the Atman exist?" (By Atman he meant a noumenon, an ego, the spiritual substance of body or soul.) Nagasena denied this existence as well.

I will continue tomorrow.

Confidence in the satori of Buddha

The second sesshin here in Val d'Isére will be over today at noon. For the beginning people in particular, I ask: What, for you, is zazen? It is Shikantaza. And also, why do we practice zazen? This we must understand. Zazen is not only for one's health, nor just for one's body. Zazen is, in particular, a problem of mind. Posture and breathing are very important. But what about our consciousness? How should that be?

Last night I said that when the body dies, its elements return to the cosmos, to the earth. The mind stays.

Our bodies do not increase or decrease. All existences continue; they do not finish. Existences change, but they do not increase or decrease.

So, to those who leave today, I will say this: During zazen one's body becomes quiet; it is like entering one's coffin. In the Dojo, during zazen, you must enter your coffin, you must die. This means that you must forget your body, you must abandon it so the mind alone stays. And in the end you will concentrate automatically, naturally, unconsciously—on consciousness, on mind. And so you will become unity with the fundamental cosmic power. This is Hishiryo-consciousness.

But you must have conviction. This is Satori; this is the Satori of the Buddha. Self-conviction. It is not necessary to think: "I have now forgotten my body, abandoned it; my body is dead. Now I must put my mind in unity with the cosmos." There is no need to think this; there is no need to think.

All the Patriarchs of the Transmission certified that zazen itself is Satori. This means that during zazen your consciousness becomes Hishiryo. This means that you become unity with the cosmic order. This is living Nirvana. You are now living, not dead. But during zazen your body is dead, forgotten, abandoned. Then the spirit, the mind, and even the dead body can become unity with the cosmos, and for eternity.

But for this you must have conviction. If you do have this conviction, and if it is a strong conviction, then you will become stronger and happier, much stronger and much happier, and you will live on into eternity—not only after death, but in this life too, as of now. Here and now your life becomes eternity. And so your condition directly before death is identical to your condition now.

After death you can live a long time—without body pain, without having to forget the ego, without having to abandon the body. In death you forget your body unconsciously, automatically, naturally. And at this time your consciousness automatically becomes unity with the cosmic power, and so you can, if you wish, live in eternity. Here and now you are living in interdependence with the ego and the cosmic power. But once this unity occurs, your karma, both the good karma and the bad, finishes. The good karma and the bad karma become ku. They enter together into the cosmic power, and so when your body dies, you yourself can still live on in eternity.

But we must have conviction. This is Satori. If we do not have conviction, all this is but knowledge. True zazen is like this. Forget the body. Leave nothing but the mind.

During zazen the body does not move. It is like the body in a coffin. And so mind-consciousness becomes strong. Mind and body activity become strong. You can feel this. Some of you feel only pain. But through correct posture and correct breathing, your mind, your consciousness, becomes one with the cosmic power.

Here is a Japanese tanka, a poem, a humorous one: "Until today I had thought it had to do only with other people; but oh, how terrible, for I too must now die!"

I hope that all of you will solve this problem of death by yourselves, here and now, and that you will find strong conviction through zazen.

Now I will chant the *Sandokai*.

∼

Last night I said that Buddha denied the existence of an Atman, of a soul. Buddha's object was for an eternal life of the spirit. He had this conviction, and so he attained true freedom.

Because your spirit returns to the cosmic power, eternal life can be realized—through conviction. This is living Nirvana. Satori is subjective conviction plus the Master's objective certification. Satori is conviction of the eternal spirit.

∼

Last zazen of this sesshin.

Concentrate! Last Satori!

T.V. cameras come today, so this zazen will finish in fifteen minutes. Then kaijo, and ceremony. So there are two more zazens. That will make double Satori [laughter].

Last kyosaku. I will give it.

OPPOSITE: *Gen no bi shoko*—Eyes horizontal, nose vertical

Session Three

August 12 – August 20, 1977

Beyond meditation

Today begins the third camp here in Val d'Isére. For beginning people, zazen is most important. You must draw your life through zazen. Eating, working, sleeping—all this must be directed by zazen. You must concentrate on all you do; even when going to the toilet you must concentrate. Zazen is not asceticism, but neither is it the Club Méditerrané. We are not here for amusement. We are here to observe ourselves, and especially our minds. We are here to find ourselves.

In daily life people think, think, think. They think with the frontal brain, and they are always very busy. Always busily thinking about their bonnos—about eating, making money, making love, and so on. But here in this camp, during your zazens, you can stop thinking with the frontal brain, and use instead the central brain. Macrocosmic thinking. Zazen means communication with the fundamental cosmic power.

Fortunately we have the fine sound of the river coming to us from in the valley. The voice of the river is giving a great sutra—the voice of cosmic truth. You can hear it—unconsciously, automatically, naturally—with your body.

∼

In zazen the posture is of highest importance. Chin in. Stretch the waist. Nose in a straight vertical line with the navel. Shoulders down. Finger position, too, is very important. Thumbs must touch, forming neither a mountain nor a valley. Concentrate on the fingers.

Breathing, too, is of utmost importance. Beginning people especially must concentrate on exhalation—long, long, long exhalation. Now concentrate on the kikai-tanden, under the navel. *Ki* means cosmic energy; *kai*, the ocean; *tanden* means field of essence of cosmic energy. If your posture is good and your concentration is on the exhalation, you obtain the cosmic energy.

Meditation has become very important in this modern civilization now in crisis. Yesterday I received a letter from a

ZEN & KARMA

Hindu monk. He writes that an important meeting is being organized in Milan between Hindus, Buddhists and Christians. The Pope has ordered it. The meeting, lasting from the thirtieth of September to the twenty-eighth of October, is then to move on to Rome. On October twentieth there is to be a congress with the Pope in the Vatican. This is a very complicated meditation reunion. The Pope has ordered that there be twelve Christian monks, two Buddhist monks, one Tibetan, and one Theravadin. I have been invited to represent Mahayana and Zen Buddhism. So I must answer them.

What is this? I cannot understand this Hindu-Tibetan-Christian meditation. I know only zazen. The Buddha chose the zazen posture, and so the separation from traditional Hindu meditation. Mahayana Zen concentrates only on zazen. Zazen is the highest meditation. It is beyond meditation.

∼

[The bell for kinhin sounds.]

Kinhin is the walking meditation, but it is not like walking. It is standing meditation, standing zazen. Kinhin is very difficult; it is more difficult than zazen.

[The bell ending Kinhin sounds.]

After kinhin you must quickly regain your zafus. I am looking to see who is last. In the other two sesshins I said that I would give a prize to the last one, but still I have not been able to decide.

Thinking in the depths of non-thinking

Concentrate under the navel. Concentrate on the exhalation. Exhalation in zazen is longer than the inhalation, and so it becomes deep and strong in the lungs. Your zazen posture must have strong dignity. Push the sky with the head, the ground with the knees. Chin in, chin in.

The position of the hands is very important. The left hand is placed on the right hand, and they rest on the foot, against the belly and under the navel. The two thumbs must be in contact. Too much pressure of thumb against thumb, or not enough pressure of thumb against thumb, is not so good. The thumbs should form the shape of an egg. Most people's thumbs here are dropping.

The thumbs and the fingers form a kind of circle directly under the kikai-tanden. *Hokai join* is the name for the position of the hands. *Hokai* means cosmos; *in* means the seal, the stamp, the symbol; *jo* means zazen.

~

I always repeat Master Dogen's words in the *Fukanzazengi*: "Think without thinking. How do we think without thinking? How do we think about non-thinking? This is beyond thinking. This is Hishiryo." Hishiryo is the secret of zazen. Zazen is the highest meditation; it is beyond meditation.

The physiology of the brain makes it so that we are always thinking with the frontal brain. In modern civilization, what with its intellectual system of education, the frontal brain has become overly developed. We think scientifically, and never do we use the interior brain, the thalamus. Animals, on the other hand, never use their frontal brains; rather, they think with the thalamus, the central brain. The central brain is the instinctive brain, the brain of nature. It is connected with the cosmic order, and so with this brain it is possible to become connected with this cosmic order. Physicians such as Dr. Paul Chauchard and Dr. Konrad Lorenz say that our civilization today is in crisis because the central brain in man has grown weak because it is sick.

The thalamus directs the body, and the hypothalamus directs the vital strength. During zazen the hormones increase within the hypothalamus, and so we become stronger. We all feel this strength within us after we have finished zazen.

[Someone has fallen unconscious and is being carried out of the Dojo by the Kyosaku-man.]

Weak people—those with a nervous sickness—when you do zazen for the first time, you will have a reaction. This is because your body and mind are returning to their natural state. It is difficult for you, but never mind. You are only returning to your natural state.

Ku, our original nature
Dogen wrote: "Don't think from thinking." This is a negation. But, "Think, not-think" is an affirmation.

In the *Shiki soku ze ku, ku soku ze shiki* of the *Hannya Shingyo*, shiki is phenomenon and it means thinking.

Ku is emptiness, and it means thinking from nonthinking.

Ku is non-thinking.

Ku is concentration.

Concentration of ku is the return of thoughts to the central brain.

Ku is the return to nature.

Ku is the originality of our nature.

Ku, which is emptiness, means consciousness of the macrocosm. And so ku is connected with the cosmic order.

We are always on one side or the other. We want freedom, we want to spread ourselves into the cosmos—by using the frontal brain. We want to realize humanity—by using the frontal brain. These are contradictions. And how do we deal with these contradictions? Dealing with these contradictions is a big problem in the world today.

The doctrine of karma and the doctrine of ku are the two essential principles of Mahayana Buddhism. They are the two pillars of Mahayana. Karma is the action created by our body, mind and words: *Ku soku ze shiki*. Emptiness becomes phenomenon. This is the affirmation. Ku is *Shiki soku ze ku*. Phenomenon becomes emptiness. This is the negation.

In daily life most people look outside; they look about objectively. Zazen means to look inside. During this sesshin you must look inside, not outside; and so you will become intimate with your own egos. Look at your ego, look at it subjectively.

What is the ego? We must look at ourselves. What is ourselves? We are the vital center of time and space. During zazen we can feel change, even though we seem changeless. During zazen we can feel our egos, our consciousness, our brains changing all the time, even though our noumenon seems changeless. Yet during daily life we do not notice these changes. What is the ego? The ego is in perpetual change. What is the noumenon of the ego? And where is it? We cannot find it. Most people feel that nature—the world, the mountains, the rivers—does not change very much. Yet during zazen we can hear the voice of the torrent changing all the time. All existences are impermanent, the ego as well. And there is no noumenon.

∼

Concentrate. The last moments in zazen are the most important. When you can no longer be patient, be patient. Then you will have deep concentration.

Realization within the everyday world

In the *Yuimakyo Sutra*,[28] Yuima came upon Sariputra sitting in zazen in the forest and he said: "Please, Sariputra, forget your body and your mind and continue zazen. Sit in the three worlds of the past, present and future, do not sit in Nirvana, and so realize that there are many postures to your dignity. Please continue your zazen, do not abandon the method of the Way, and so realize the natural and personal posture. Please, Sariputra, continue your zazen, but do not cut off the bonnos so that you may enter into living Nirvana."

This criticism of Sariputra shows Yuima's attitude concerning ku. The attitude of ku is the complete, the proper zazen. True zazen, true Nirvana, in Yuima's opinion, is its realization in our daily life of bonnos. True zazen, true meditation, does not exist without a relationship, without an interdependence, between it and bonnos. Maybe Sariputra was searching for the state of

---

[28]   *Yuimakyo Sutra*: Also known as the *Vimalakirti Nirdesa Sutra*.

absolute Nirvana when Yuima came upon him in the forest. (This state of absolute Nirvana is identical to transcendental or holy wisdom, and it is beyond the realm of illusions in the three worlds. The state of true Satori, on the other hand, is reflected and conveyed from within the center of the vulgar world of bonnos.) Sariputra had simply forgotten that true Mahayana Buddhism is here and now—*Bonno soku Bodai*[29]—and so Yuima's criticism of Sariputra.

True living Nirvana does not exist in the world of purification, nor beyond the realm of dirt. True living Nirvana is reflected and conveyed from within the center of our daily lives, even from within the worst of daily lives, from within those times and those places where the voice of the devil is heard, and not that of the Dharma, from where there is but disbelief in the Buddha's teachings, from where there is doubt for all the sacred teachings. This is the real way of Mahayana Buddhism. This is the Middle Way. Be not attached.

The *Yuimakyo Sutra* continues as follows: "The beautiful lotus flower does not grow in the fresh and pure fields, nor on the mountaintops; the beautiful lotus grows in the low places, where there is mud." And again: "Without entering into the ocean of bonnos we would never obtain the treasure of absolute wisdom."

True living Nirvana is not to be found in special monasteries, nor in mountain retreats for ascetics. Living Nirvana is itself our bonnos and our karma; this is its source. Any concept of Satori, Buddha or God removed from our daily lives is abstraction, and so Buddha or God becomes but a mere abstract doll.

So I say to you, even if you wear a suit, wear long hair, and grow a beard, please continue zazen. Have right views and right behavior. Even if you live in family life, do not become attached to the vulgar world. Even if you live with your wife and children, find pleasure in solitude. Even if you obtain much vulgar profit, do not feel joy from it. You must have compassion for all people,

---

[29] *Bonno soku Bodai*: Bonno becomes Satori (Truth).

Session Three: August 12 – August 20, 1977

play with them and work with them. When I was a child I always sang this song—but I will sing it for you tomorrow. Time is almost up.

Concentrate on your exhalation. Then you will not jump at the sound of the loud drum. Concentrate this way and your kikai-tanden will become strong.

Transforming illusions
During zazen we can see, we can feel our bodies entering into the world of death. The mind becomes solitary, as if it has gone off to a far away place. We do not experience this in daily life because we move too much. In zazen, with the muscles in tension, we forget the body. This state—of the spirit and of the body—is the state of living Nirvana. So, if at this moment you are in front of death, then you see that to face death is not so difficult. Do not think, be not scared, be not attached, forget everything, and you will enter straightaway into the world of death. Please try. Close your eyes. We observe our lives, past and present, our karma, our problems with family, with money, we observe that which frightens us, our anxieties, but they are no longer so important.

∼

Now I will continue last night's kusen.

Last night I said that the true nature of ku is awakened within the bonnos. True Satori is conveyed, reflected in the bonnos. It is within the bonnos where Satori is to be realized. The ice of bonnos becomes the water of Nirvana. But the problem is: How should we use our bonnos? How can we change our karma? If we use bonno for bonno, we perpetuate our bad karma. We create, then, that which is called transmigration.

∼

When I was a child I always sang this song:

> *Don't be defeated by the rain. Don't be defeated by the wind. Don't be defeated by the snow. And so in the heat of summertime.*
>
> *Be of healthy body, without desire, without anger, and smile always. Eat but guenmai rice, miso soup, and some vegetables. Be free from grasping and obtaining, practice concentration, have a strong memory, and be not forgetful.*
>
> *I would like to live in a little straw-roofed house in the shadow of the pines in the plain. And if to the east of where I live there is a sick child, I will go and help him. If in the west a tired mother works, I will go and help and I will massage her shoulders. If in the south a man is dying, I will go to him and tell him not to worry and not to be afraid of death, and if he were to die, I would cry with compassion for him and his family. If in the north there is a quarrel, I will go and tell them to stop it, for there is no profit in quarreling.*
>
> *If some criticize me and treat me as a foolish boy, I will not be sad. If others admire me and say that I am good, I will not be happy about it. I hope to be a boy like this.*

This is a Japanese children's song of the provinces. Its influence was Mahayana Buddhism. It is a Bodhisattva song for the education of children.

∽

There is no cutting off of bonnos in Mahayana Buddhism. Rather, one must refine bonnos to a higher dimension. We must jump into the bonnos—and use them for the benefit of others.

But this can be dangerous if one's viewpoint is mistaken. "I always help women with my bonnos—by making love to them." Or: "I always help men—I always open my sex to them." This has nothing to do with the Bodhisattva way. What these people say is untrue.

Session Three: August 12 – August 20, 1977

Here is a short verse by the great Nembutsu Master Shinran: "Sin and karma become the body of charity and virtue." This is similar to the image of ice which becomes water. The more ice, the more water. The more bonnos, the bigger the Satori, and so the more deeply one can attain living Nirvana.

I, too, wrote a poem here in Val d'Isére:

During the sesshin in the mountains of Val d'Isere,
The sound of the valley, the color of the mountains,
Everything is the mind of God.
So I observe my mind with nature.

∽

Don't move! You must not move before the sound of the Kaijo, nor before the other bells. Only when you place your Kesas on your heads can you move.

The kaijo indicates the hour. In Japanese temples a big bell also does the same. But here, as we have no hanging bell, the kaijo is followed by the striking of the wood.

A strong education

This camp, which lasts ten days, cost you 780 francs. This is not so expensive as some think. Places here in Val d'Isére are very expensive to rent, and besides I am giving you a strong education, a historic education. So you too must give a *fuse* [gift]. Yet some here are always criticizing the price. The second sesshin was the worst. Someone stole money from behind the bar. I want to use the financial profits for my mission in the future. Money is necessary today. But no one helps me. No government gives me money. And I receive none from Japan. I have no financial protector, no supporter. Other religions have plenty.

Today I ordered the rensaku for four people. When you make mistakes during a sesshin, I must give you the rensaku. Each Kyosaku-man will give you ten strikes per shoulder. The rensaku is difficult to give, so I must have two accurate and strong Kyosaku-men. Men, not women. Michel! Stephane! You give the rensakus. And give them strongly.

When you are about to receive the rensaku, there is no need to first do gassho.

This is not the Club Méditerrané. In China, in Japan, sesshins are very strong. But me, I am soft. My education is soft. Of course, for beginning people all this is very difficult. But with the older disciples I must be strong. I must strongly educate my disciples.

Sometimes, during the days of preparation before the sesshin, I do not eat with you, and sometimes I do not come for the afternoon zazens. This is because I want to see how my older disciples educate and prepare the others. But today I came down to lunch unexpectedly and discovered that four of my very important disciples had escaped without permission. It is possible to go out from the retreat, but with permission. Still, my closest disciples must remain and represent me when I am not here.

The rensaku, this time, is for A., E., R., and MJ.

E. is my top disciple, and he has been with me the longest. If he makes mistakes, then everyone will make mistakes. If I die now, you, E., must continue![30]

Kyosaku-men! Give the rensaku strongly. Don't be diplomatic.

[The Kyosaku-men begin administering the rensaku.]

Stronger! Stronger![31]

---

[30] See photo insert section for picture of Deshimaru with E. (Etienne Zeisler).

[31] Nowadays, the rensaku is hardly ever given—the times have changed, the practionners suffer less from physical pain and disturb others much less than before. At Deshimaru's time, people behaved often irresponsibly and it was not always easy for the master to maintain the right conditions for the practice. In this particular situation he reacts so strongly because some of his closest disciples, on whom he much counted, were indeed wild and undisciplined.

About cause and effect: not so obvious
The new people who have come for this sesshin should read the printed kusens so they will understand better. Both hearing my kusens and then reading them later is important. When you hear them during zazen, you hear them with your body, and at this time a powerful seed is planted in the neurons of the central brain, and so you develop a strong karma. When you read these kusens, you understand them intellectually.

∼

Shakti is the fundamental impulsion of the cosmos. The concept of Shakti, which dates back to traditional Indian thought, was transformed by the Buddha and enlarged in scope to include the source of all personal acts. Action, in Buddhism, is therefore the relationship existing between the cause and the effect of karma. As to the karmic effects, there are good and bad effects or, more accurately, liked and disliked effects.

Shakti in Buddhism is *Kalitra*, and Kalitra means the effect. (Kalitra also has two other meanings which I will explain shortly.) What is effect? Effect can mean the action which produces the effect—*jnana*[32] in Sanskrit. Effect here can also mean the action which influences (but does not produce) the effect—*Aksapa* in Sanskrit.

The action which produces the effect is a direct cause, and so it is called contagious. The action which influences the effect is realized through En (interdependence), and so it is called infectious.

Most people believe that karma comes about through a contagious cause. They are wrong. The cause of karma is infectious, not contagious.

As I said in the first sesshin, the effect is the result produced by the action, and this in itself necessitates many varying

---

[32] *Jnana*: Wisdom, higher intellect, sometimes worldly knowledge.

conditions. Yet in the science of causality it is claimed that one cause produces one effect, and, likewise, that the cause of karma is contagious. So you can see that the science of causality is not really rational. It is abstract. The doctrine of karma, on the other hand, is very scientific—more so than science itself. If people were to truly understand the doctrine of karma, science would advance with great and rapid strides.

A monk has asked me to sing a sutra this morning, so now I will sing the *Sandokai*.

Behavior and consciousness

I will now continue the kusen on the karmic system.

This morning I explained that the Hindu word Shakti, which is the traditional Indian doctrine of the cosmos, means, in Buddhism, the fundamental power—Kalitra—or karma. Kalitra means the effect, or the effect of the action, as I have already explained. Kalitra also means ceremony.

Ceremony. What does ceremony mean? In Russia, it came to mean a conditioned reflex—as according to Pavlov. In France, we have what is called "the structure of behavior"—as according to Merleau-Ponty. In America, ceremony has come to mean behavior or manners—as according to Watson and his doctrine of modern behaviorism. Now, Merleau-Ponty is a critic of Pavlov's conditioned reflex, and Konrad Lorenz is a critic of Watson's behaviorism.

Modern behaviorism bases itself simply upon objective observation—that is, on psychological and objective consciousness. Though both these are necessary, it is nonetheless difficult to make a science out of this, because it still remains one-sided. There is no true subjective reflection in behaviorism.

In Buddhism we have Shikantaza, which is observation and concentration while looking on the inside, and which becomes Hishiryo-consciousness. However, as each person's Hishiryo-consciousness is different, scientific analysis of this state is very difficult to come by. In Buddhism we also have what is called behaviorism. The posture is objective. We push the ground with the head—no, that is Yoga—here we push the head with the head—no, I am making a mistake—we push the sky with the head, and we push the ground with the knees. This is behaviorism.

As to the ceremony, we repeat it every day. Every day, after zazen, we chant the *Hannya Shingyo*. We repeat the sampais, and so on. The ceremony is objective. It is behavior; it has to do with mannerisms.

Our behavior influences our consciousness. And, of course, our consciousness influences our behavior. Behavior can therefore change our consciousness. Bad behavior and bad manners influence our brains, the action of our bodies, our words, our conversation, and so our karma.

But as our consciousness also influences our behavior, in Zen we always continue our meditational practices with internal observation and concentration. And this is not behaviorism. So in Zen there is both the subjective in zazen and the objective in the ceremony. Master Dogen wrote very extensively on how we must go to the toilet, and how we should eat—*Dokan*.[33] So this is ceremony, the second definition of the word Kalitra.

Kalitra has three meanings. It can mean the effect or the effect of the action, as I explained this morning. It can mean ceremony. And finally it can mean the effect of karma. More precisely, Kalitra can mean the effect of desirable-undesirable karma.

When we say desirable or undesirable, we do not mean good or bad. This does not have to do with a moral judgment. A moral judgment is an objective judgment, whereas what we are talking about here is a subjective judgment. If we do a good thing, our karma in the future is good—not in the moral sense, but rather in the sense of a karma that is loved. The effect which appears is one we like, we love; so therefore this is not a moral problem, but rather a personal psychological problem.

---

[33] *Dokan*: The ring of the Way. The continual repetition of the acts of one's daily life—waking up, zazen, meals, work, toilet, going to bed, etc.—all becomes Dokan, the ring of the Way. See Glossary.

Karma is not affected by changing social orders, by national customs, by governmental laws, by changing times. Contrarily, moral judgments depend upon these factors. Fundamental morals, however, always remain the same. Don't kill, don't steal, and so on. The problem of karma is that it is influenced by potential phenomena, and so it is not determined by moral judgment. As, for instance, the case where we want to do good but cannot; or, likewise, when we want to do bad but cannot. Karma does not have to do with good or bad. There is no good or bad karma, good or bad effect. Karma is subjective.

So I repeat: The system of karma is of three sorts—action, ceremony or behavior, and effects liked or disliked.

Zazen, objectively certified?

Zazen itself is not behaviorism. Yet it is possible to certify zazen objectively. Physiologically speaking we can talk of the zazen posture, of the muscular tension, of the electrical current of the alpha waves which appear during zazen, of the diaphragm which drops during the exhalation and which massages the interior organs, of the blood circulation which becomes more active. We can talk of the influence the zazen posture has on the brain; of how, when the frontal brain rests, the central brain becomes active; and of the hypothalamus which becomes stronger. All this is certified by science. But certification by science and certification by psychology do not prove much. Though we may be certified objectively by science, zazen is not a science and so we must have subjective certification. Yet it is not possible to subjectively certify each and every one of us separately. Someone says: "I've got Satori!" If he says this, then it is not true; it is not real Satori. When a madman says: "I am normal!" it is not true and no one believes him. And because no one believes him, a doctor is called in to certify his statement.

Anyway, zazen is within the domain of the religious, and not limited within the dimensions of psychology, physiology or

OPPOSITE: *Shin fuka toku*—Mind cannot be grasped

心得不可

竹禪仙

science. So in the end it is the Master who certifies. Every day the Master certifies. "You are doing zazen, so automatically, unconsciously and naturally you get Satori," he says. The Master watches you from behind, and in the end, he gives you the Shiho.

Karma, a subjective problem
The word "world" can mean the world of nature, the world of man, the world of the personal or of the spiritual. There are many worlds. But in Buddhism the world—*seken*—means only the personal world. The kanji *sekai* means world, and though the word seken is also defined in the dictionary as "world," seken means the human world only—*Loka* in Sanskrit. So sekai and seken have different meanings. Karma does not have to do with sekai, but only with seken. Seken means destruction, impermanence. Seken does not have to do with the natural sciences.

The traditional Indian religion, in turning too much toward the cosmos, forgot humanity. The Hindu, living in the big deserts and in the Himalayas, always tended toward the imagination. But in the Buddha's time true humanity was discovered—by the Buddha himself. And so the traditional Indian religion, transformed into a religion of humanism, discovered the true humanity of Buddhism. (The humanism which developed in Europe during the Renaissance turned against God.)

Nonetheless, karma, with its causes and effects, cannot be limited by the natural sciences. It is limited by the seken world. Karma is a spiritual and subjective problem, and so it has to do with the personal world, the world of seken. Karma is always moving. It is always impermanent. It rises and falls; it increases and decreases; it is impermanence and it is vicissitude, as with the world of seken.

~

Today, after lunch, begins *Hosan* for one and a half days. *Ho* means free and *san* means to receive the Master's teaching; so Hosan means to be free from doing zazen. In Japan a sign saying "Hosan" is placed at the entrance to the Dojo. It means holiday. Nonetheless, those in charge here must do samu, even during Hosan.

A poem to go beyond language
The postures of zazen and kinhin are simply the normal condition of the human being. If you are not normal, these two postures will be very difficult, especially during the early morning zazen.

[Someone has fallen unconscious and is now being helped out of the Dojo by the Kyosaku-man.]

Some of you even fall down. But never mind. Continue zazen and kinhin and you will come back to the normal condition.

During zazen the position of the eyes is very important. Rest the eyes one meter in front of you on the ground. Don't move them. Don't fix them either. Not too open, not too closed. Some people's eyes here are wide open and empty—like the eyes of a dog after he has had sex. Empty eyes are no good.

∽

[The Master recites a poem in Japanese.]

This poem was written by Sotoba, who was famous in ancient China and a great Bodhisattva. He got Satori from the color of the mountains and the sound of the river in the valley. And so we have this poem about the voice of the valley; a long and large tongue is giving a conference, a conference by the Buddha. The clean pure body of the Buddha is the color of the mountains . . . Look at the color of the French Alps—it is this. The color of mountains is not like the color of buildings. And so Sotoba woke up by the color of the mountains and the voice of the river. The sound of the river of Val d'Isére that we hear now during zazen is not the same as the sound of a machine. The sound of the valley is the sound of nature. This river here has made 84,000 poems since midnight. How can I convey to you this great conference? By phrases and by kanjis? By a poem? It is very difficult. It is very difficult to express the true truth through language. Language makes categories.

Subjective observation during zazen is different with each person. Now in this Dojo there are more than two hundred people, and each one's thinking is different. What are you thinking? Hishiryo-thinking, now. If one took a photograph of you at this moment, the posture would be captured, but not the attitude of the mind.

In one of Master Dogen's poems it is written: "The color of the mountain, the echo of the valley, everything is the posture and the mind of Shakyamuni Buddha." And so it is the same with the posture and mind of God. It is the posture of the mind of zazen. It is zazen-mind. [Silence.]

During the early morning zazen many of you become sleepy. At this hour there are still traces of dreams. Many also sleep during the afternoon zazen. And so with the night zazen. All they want to do during the night zazen is to go to bed. There are others who fall asleep whenever they get into the posture. Then there are those who simply sleep all the time, from morning until night. But *kontin*[34] during zazen is better than its opposite, *sanran*. Those who are too nervous, as in sanran, sometimes fall down during zazen. This is what happens when you are too nervous. Nonetheless, sleepiness and nervousness are not normal conditions. If you are in either kontin or sanran, you must ask for the kyosaku. Receive the kyosaku and your mind will completely change. Kyosaku means the stick which promotes Satori. It is the stick which wakes you up—the wake-up stick. There are now three Kyosaku-men. You, Kyosaku-men, you must not stick together in the same place. On the right side of the Dojo there are no Kyosaku-men.

Kaijo!

---

[34] *Kontin*: Sleepiness.

Session Three: August 12 – August 20, 1977

Understanding the conditions of our existence
In our social system there exist moral laws, and there exist social morals. Sometimes the honest worker becomes destitute, and the dishonest man becomes a rich and important minister. The man walking on the right path receives disagreeable effects. The bad receive the good, the good the bad. Why is this so? Social morals are limited and cannot solve these problems. Nor can they be solved by philosophy. Rather, they can be solved through religion. For these problems are problems of karma. Karma is an analytic fact. It cannot be used to the advantage of the social opportunist.

Socrates talks about right living, and he says that man should live rightly. But what is right living, correct living, just living? In Greece? In the Orient? What is considered just in Greece is not the same as what is considered just in the Orient. The standards of what is good and of what is bad are, in the end, not so very clear. For the standards of what is good or bad depend upon place, custom and time. And so we can see how social morals are not so very exact.

How we live our lives has to do with how we understand karma. Our lives are simply a continuation of karma itself. Though karma is beyond causality, if we analyze and observe our karma, we can understand the real condition of our lives. Karma is infinite, but it is not abstract philosophy. In Buddhism true good is the contented feeling we have in our inside minds when, for example, we do a fuse for the Buddha, for the monks, or for others.

Merits beyond gain and loss
And vice versa. "Good" in Sanskrit is *ksara*, and "bad" is *aksara*. To feel discontented, unhappy, displeased in our inside mind is *aksara*. When a man has sex with another's wife, or a wife with another's husband, they experience satisfaction and maybe joy. But this satisfaction is not an effect of karma. However, in the future they will receive an effect of karma and it will be a bad effect. It will be bad karma. One must always consider one's

actions in the light of one's future. Which is more pleasant, the joys of the present or the pain of the future? Today we are happy, tomorrow we suffer. So we must not rejoice over our little joys; we must see that in the future it will bring us much pain and suffering. Zazen is painful, it is here-and-now painful. The local people in Val d'Isére see us doing zazen and they see it as painful and stupid. They have had no experience with zazen, and so they are skeptical. "Why do they sit like that, without moving? It is so painful. Really, it is a waste of time."

But the karma from doing zazen will bring good effects in the future. The highest. Dogen wrote in the *Shobogenzo* that one obtains the highest effects, the greatest karma, from doing zazen. This is true—from zazen we receive infinite effects in the future. Yet we must not do zazen for its effects. We must be Mushotoku—without object. Why do I say this? Because then you will truly attain the highest effects, and your karma in the future will be infinite.

[Someone is being led out of the Dojo by the Kyosaku-man.]

Those who have a hardness in their muscles and tendons have sick muscles and tendons. So sitting in zazen they feel this sickness. They feel the pain. But if they continue this sesshin, sitting in the correct posture, three times a day for the next ten days, their muscles, their tendons will return to normal. Zazen is the strongest of auto-massages.

Three minutes more. If you wait for the bell, the time seems long. But if you concentrate on your breathing, time passes.

Karma produces nothing of itself

Today I will give a kusen on the influence and power of karma.

As I have explained, karma is infectious, not contagious. Karma itself cannot produce effects. The cause of karma is the cause which helps another cause.

A man is committed to charity and yet he is poor and he suffers. Or a dishonest man becomes rich. This is because the power of past karma influences the present. Likewise, the man who never practiced charity in the past is today stingy. One's actions in the present are a realization of one's past karma. One's past karma is the action of the present.

However, karmically speaking, ancestors of the past do not influence their offspring. The curse of ancestors does not become karma. The past of ancestors does not return to haunt their children of today, for a man only receives the effects of his own karma and not that of others. The power of karma has no influence on others. The power of karma is the power which helps the cause, and so no relationship exists between one's own karma and the karma of another. All karma is subjective and psychological, so how could it become something subjective for someone else?

But the power of karma is not so weak. Karma cannot create, but it has the power to grow. Karma is not creative power; it is growing power.

To produce means to create. To produce is the power of creation. But as with a seed which cannot germinate all by itself, the power of help, the power to join in, is also necessary. Dirt, water, sun and the correct temperature are needed for this seed to germinate. And this is the power of karma—the power which helps the cause. To make a car, iron, plastic, copper and an engine are necessary, but if people do not produce these materials then a car cannot be made. Material alone cannot produce a car; people must produce it. Spiritual action is necessary. Natural power is necessary.

So this is not a contagious power—it is an infectious one. This is very important. The germinating of a seed, the work of man in making a car are infectious powers, not contagious. In German the word *Einbildungskraft* means that which combines, joins, including the many elements, conditions, variations from the past, the present and the future.

Non-manifested karma is like a seed

The power of karma does not belong to the material. Karma is moving; it is alive. Its substance is internal, and it belongs to the activity of the consciousness. And so it becomes the élan vital—the vital thrust—the cause which helps the cause.

In modern times the criminal is more and more common. Criminal minds increase, laws increase, and all becomes more complicated. This is the karma of civilization. Our action is manifested objectively, and it is situated in time; it has potential in the moment, but when the action is completed, then there is nothing. In legal terms, in moral terms, once the action is terminated, the problem no longer exists, so it is something superficial. If one kills, steals—the two hundred francs from behind the bar, for example—it is only the action itself which becomes the issue, for if the person escapes, if the thief cannot be found, then it is finished. People forget. The police too. But from the viewpoint of religion, the action committed does not finish. Once the action has been committed, the seed is there, and so it remains. According to the doctrine of karma, the seed is not eternal, but remains only until the time of death. In the living person, however, the seed is there—in the roots of the action. So a thief released from prison robs again. The crime is repeated. It is habitual. So it is with the killer, or with the sexually obsessed. One, two, three, four different men—and the woman becomes a vamp. The man, a Don Juan. Because the seed remains. One cannot simply stop this by the use of willpower, or through the fear of the police, or by prison, because the karma existing here is nonmanifest. In psychological terms this is called the subconscious.

Mushogo in Japanese means the nonmanifest karma, the internal, unseen karma. It is like vibrations or the codes of a sound. So the seed remains . . . Of course, if the nonmanifest karma is weaker than the will, then it is sometimes possible to kill this seed through willpower. But such a seed cannot generally be stopped in this way. And it certainly cannot be stopped by the law, nor by existing moral codes.

So, how can we stop this nonmanifest karma? By what method? Buddhism has a very deep solution to this problem, and this is why the doctrine of karma is very important in

Buddhism. Through voluntarism, on the other hand, it is very difficult to check this bad seed, this bad habit of the personality. Nonmanifest karma is not realized on the surface; it is realized very deeply within oneself. (Of course, everybody is different, and while some have a deep-rooted karma, others do not.)

If a candle is blown out, the flame stops. The burning flame is similar to manifest action—as of the body and the mind. And so, at this moment, the acts of sex, stealing and killing come to an end. But the candle still remains, and so does the body, and so do the crimes. The nonmanifest karma still exists. Likewise with a storm. The storm stops, and so do the waves in the sea and on the beach. But the sea remains.

The manifest karma is manifested, it is experienced, and then it ends. But the invisible power still remains, and this invisible power is Mushogo or nonmanifest karma. And this karma is continued in the next action—for this karma controls and manages the coming action. Because these seeds are in the consciousness, nonmanifest karma can reproduce the same action again and again.

The body wants to stop this action, and so does the mind, and it tries to do so with the will. But it cannot, because the seed is buried deep in the central brain. The seed is out of reach of the frontal brain, and so it cannot be controlled by the frontal brain.

Zazen's influence on karma

But nonmanifest karma is not a solitary phenomenon. The action of nonmanifest karma is the action of the body and of the mouth. It is a creation of the body and of the mouth. Just as the shadow of a tree depends upon the tree, nonmanifest karma depends upon manifest karma. Now, if the tree does not move, the shadow does not move. Once, in a mondo which has become famous in the history of Zen, the Sixth Patriarch, Eno, was discussing the movement of a flag with some monks and a nun.

"The flag is moving."

"No, the flag is not moving. It is the wind which moves."

"No, it is the mind which moves. It is consciousness which moves."

"No," cut in the great nun. "Everything is moving—the flag, the wind, the mind."

Here is a very important point. This shows the relationship between manifest and nonmanifest karma. Between body-and-mind and nonmanifest karma. Between the tree and the shadow. What comes first, the body or the interior mind? The relationship here is one of interdependence.

It is described in the *Shobogenzo* by Master Dogen how one day, while Master Hotetsu was fanning himself, a monk came up to him and said: "Since air is everywhere, why do you use a fan?" (A foolish mondo, this—but interesting. The monk just wanted to have a discussion with the Master. It is the same here during mondos. People just want to have discussions with the Master, so they create and produce all kinds of complicated questions.)

Anyway, Hotetsu replied: "You alone know that the wind exists everywhere. What you do not know is that without practice we cannot create and produce it. Without using the fan we cannot create and produce the wind."

Practice zazen, practice the posture, the proper breathing, the silence of the mouth—for all this influences the body. If you think zazen is painful, then it will be painful. If your body is in pain, then so will be your consciousness.

If you practice zazen in a Dojo with many others, then your nonmanifest karma will become good. A good, infinite, nonmanifest karma. If you do zazen in a Dojo with many others, it will become a habit, and so even if you have bad karma, the nonmanifest karma of your zazen will strengthen you, and then you will be able to control your bad nonmanifest karma. Even if you are sexually obsessed, this obsession will diminish.

Those who have bad karma are always impatient, and they are the first to move. This moving creates bad karma for the others.

[Someone is being helped out of the Dojo by the Kyosaku-man.]

It is always the same ones who fall down. It is their nonmanifest karma appearing.

Session Three: August 12 – August 20, 1977

Editor's Note: *Though it might appear to the reader that the people here are falling like flies, it should be kept in mind that during these thirty-six days in Val d'Isére, over a thousand people, and many of them new to the practice, attended one or more of the four camp periods. That some of them experienced certain psycho-physiological difficulties is, after all, hardly surprising.*

When a tree falls its shadow disappears

Kyosaku-men are not to give the stick during the kusen. Just correct postures. To wake up the sleepers, poke them in the lower back with the kyosaku, at the level of their fifth vertebra.

∼

All night long poems are being created; 84,000 of them are produced from the torrent. But how can I explain them? Last night I made up another poem about this river here in Val d'Isére, and now I turn my head and reflect about the past, about my last ten years in France, about the good and the bad, about that which has been obtained, and about that which has been lost. It is a dream.

The mountain in August, the sound of the stream, the sound of the torrent in the valley—at midnight it enters, it fills the empty window, the solitary window.

∼

Some Buddhists say that karma continues after death. But this is not so. The nonmanifest karma (Mushogo) does not continue after death. It does not enter the world of death. When we die, nonmanifest karma comes to an end. When the tree falls, the shadow disappears.

There is another Buddhist issue, a more philosophic one, which says that the doctrine of nonmanifest karma is in contradiction to the doctrine of vanishing phenomena. The doctrine of vanishing phenomena explains that all phenomena are illusion, imagination, catching only the moment. Vanishing, they have no reality. This is the true, real aspect of all existences which are in change. We call this the continuing moment—of the past, the present, the future. The present moment cannot be caught, and since this is so, nonmanifest karma too is real. So there appears to be a contradiction between the reality of nonmanifest karma and the doctrine of vanishing phenomena (the doctrine of moment-after-moment vanishing). But what is reality? In Buddhism, reality is the existence of each separate being. Not just affirmed existence, but also negative nonexistence. So therefore, there is no difference between the two doctrines. There is no contradiction existing between the reality of nonmanifest karma and the reality of vanishing, the reality of the disappearedness of each moment.

Cutting the root of karma
Another issue: the relationship between karma and samsara. They are not the same; they are different. And this is why the Buddha denied samsara: because the echo of nonmanifest karma cannot decide, it cannot determine the after-death.

The power of the subconscious, found in modern psychology, is the same as the doctrine of karma. But the doctrine of karma goes deeper. Surface karma, manifested by the body, becomes a habit—like an echo or a vibration—and so it influences one's interior actions, causing the creation of good karma to stop—and so this is nonmanifest karma of the body. So it is, too, with karma of the mouth, or of the word. Create bad words, speak bad things, and when you want to speak good things, the bad spoken words will still be there, hidden unconsciously by the power of karma. *Fushogo* in Japanese is the nonmanifest karma of words. Anyway, this analysis is easy to understand. Modern psychology as well has solved and certified all this.

Some people here think that Sensei has forgotten the hour. Some are in zazen-hell. I can tell by the movement of their

OPPOSITE: *Chiku Ju*—The wind in the bamboo forest

中风

buttocks. Some are more accurate than a clock. After exactly thirty minutes their buttocks move. So when I want to know the time, all I do is look at their buttocks. It is their nonmanifest karma arising. Karma is very exact.

Kyosaku-men are not to give the kyosaku. But they are not to walk about like phantoms either. Examine postures. Examine . . .

∿

At death, nonmanifest karma is finished. So, as to Laurent's question during the mondo: "How can we cut the root of non-manifest karma?" I answer that if you die you can cut it. This is the best method. Another method for cutting it is through the practice of zazen. If your mind is as in death (this is zazen—Hishiryo-consciousness—living Nirvana), then you can cut your nonmanifest karma. This is not an answer to how to cut non-manifest karma, but just a method. If, during zazen, your nonmanifest karma arises, since you do not move, nothing can come of it. Even the sexually obsessed at most can only ejaculate on their zafus—they can't make love.

Modern psychologists say that were a method developed which could cut out the subconscious, it would be a great discovery—greater than the plane or than the atom bomb. Such a method, they say, would be a great discovery for the advancement of mankind.

Zazen has already made this discovery. The Masters of the Transmission did not know of this discovery, but I know. They did not know of this because they did not know psychology. Dogen did not know psychology either. So the Masters tried to explain it all through poems and through literature. Difficult, this. But through psychology and physiology it is easy to explain the process. Hishiryo? What is that? I don't know.

During zazen sometimes we think, sometimes we don't. Dogen, in the *Fukanzazengi*, said: "What is Hishiryo? It is thinking about non-thinking. Thinking without thinking. Not-thinking about thinking."

It is both. When we are not hearing, we are hearing. This is the subconscious.

Thoughts come from the thalamus like dreams. You dream while in bed, and tiredness in the brain is dispersed. We dream, we sleep, and we dream again. Those in good health do not recall their dreams. So the tired brain rests. But this problem cannot be resolved simply through dreams. For in daily life we still remain anxious.

If you do zazen, then automatically, unconsciously and naturally your subconscious will arise. I am always telling you not to stop your subconscious from arising. So, after these ten days of zazen, your subconscious thoughts will have ended. And when the sesshin is over and you are having your last lunch here, your faces will be relaxed and happy—no doubt because you can now leave. But also you will be happy because your subconscious has finished.

∼

If you continue sitting in zazen for a long time, the attachments you have in your daily lives will become more apparent.

Some people sleep. That's all they ever do. Others concentrate—on the sound of the torrent below the Dojo, or on the pair of buttocks in front of them. But let all these things pass, pass, pass . . . More things, more thoughts, will arise, but soon they too will pass on. They will no longer be of much importance

In Japan, after the morning zazen, the *Sandokai* and *Hokyo Zan Mai* are chanted in original Chinese. Then the kaijo. The powerful sound of the kaijo influences the kikai-tanden, making it stronger. Sounds during zazen are very effective.

Non-manifested karma

Yesterday I spoke about nonmanifest karma. There exist two teachings on this subject. One, that there is no nonmanifest karma in the mind. The other, that there is nonmanifest karma in the mind—and more there than anywhere else.

If, during zazen, we let our thoughts pass, pass, so that there remains no trace of them at all, if no thoughts stay in our thinking, if no resting on them exists, then this mind—which is always changing, like a monkey—will have no nonmanifest karma in it.

But if in our thinking we create bonnos, if we become attached to our thoughts, then the traces left over by them will influence the neurons in our frontal and central brains—all this has been certified through scientific research—and they will become nonmanifest karma in our minds. If we have a grudge against someone, and if, unable to forget this grudge, we hold onto it, we think about it, then it will become a great bonno of attachment. And so it will become nonmanifest karma.

The substance of karma is thinking. How we think here and now—this is very important. "Think about nonthinking," said Dogen. "Don't think about thinking." How does one not-think about thinking? This is Hishiryo. This is the secret of zazen.

The kanji *shi* in Japanese means thinking—*Setana* in Sanskrit. In original Sanskrit, *set* means to pile up, to accumulate. To accumulate good or bad karma.

So karma means thinking. When we accumulate thinking, it becomes karma. When we do not accumulate thinking—that is, when we think but once about something—then it does not become karma. During zazen the subconscious arises, and so the thoughts therein do not become karma. When the subconscious comes out, karma vanishes.

When we think, we create an object for our thinking, and so we have objective thinking. Descartes is famous for having said, "I think; therefore, I am."

I say, "I don't think; therefore, I am." Both are necessary. "Sometimes I think and sometimes I don't; therefore, I am." So, [the concept of] this last statement, along with zazen, are both necessary. The French are big thinkers. Pascal once said that man is a *roseau pensant*. Anyway, the French thinker Maine de Biran later rectified the thinking of Descartes by saying, "I act; therefore, I exist." This statement is more fully developed, and it is closer to zazen.

Session Three: August 12 – August 20, 1977

"I speak; therefore, I am." No one has said this yet. Man is thinking, and the *roseau* is speaking. Many people speak. They are always speaking. Right after the morning *Bussho Kapila*[35] they speak. Some even continue to speak while sleeping in bed.

When we suffer, when we are afraid, when we are angry, when we are full of hate or of desire, we think. We think about it. Even during zazen. Yesterday, during the mondo, a woman asked me how we think about suffering in Zen. A deep question, a deep problem.

What is the object of suffering? If we do not understand the object of suffering, we cannot cut suffering.

A madam here has just moved her hips, so now I must stop. She is accurate—time to stop. Kinhin!

∿

[The bell is struck and everyone stands up and begins kinhin.]

In kinhin the backbone must be straight, the eyes must rest three meters before you on the lower back of the person in front of you. Chin in. Stretch the neck. Stretch the knee of the leg in front of you. Leave the other leg relaxed, without tension.

[The bell is again struck and all return to their places.]

∿

In Buddhism the doctrine of cosmic existentialism has as its object the Dharma. What is Dharma? That all existences are in interdependent relationship—this is Dharma. Sometimes our personal thinking follows the cosmic order; sometimes our thinking opposes this order. Most people, during zazen, follow this order. Hishiryo is to follow the cosmic consciousness. In German philosophy, Rosenburg uses the term *Akt der Erweiterung*,

---

[35] *Bussho Kapila*: The mealtime sutra the group recites together before breakfast and sometimes before lunch.

and this means that our acts make up part of the fundamental cosmic order. Human experience, writes Rosenburg, is the relationship between the ego (the interior mind), and the outside phenomena (outside surroundings). And at that moment, when this relationship exists, both are momentarily connected. It is not necessary to question the reality of the sun when you look at it. The sun, which exists in movement, consists of many elements. But of the sun's substance [of its noumenon] we do not know. So when we look at the sun, we are merely looking at an illusion. Likewise with the ego. There is no relationship between the ego and the sun, because, like the sun, ego has no substance, no noumenon. In fact, no reality. So, between our world and the human being there exist infinite connections of infinite elements through the existence of interrelationships and by the multitudinous combinations of phenomena. As I have said, many causes make many effects.

The structure of the world in which people live is made up of a composition of phenomena, of a combination of objects and of people. So how do we cut karma? How do we create good karma? A big problem, this. In becoming the source of fundamental power, our will—our consciousness—determines our actions and our words.

Nature, action and the cosmic order

Sometimes we act first; at other times we speak before we act. Many people speak before they act. Some women here speak right away on seeing the faces of their friends. Then there are people who speak in order to criticize others. Or to criticize the food on the table: "Only couscous! Never any meat. And look at the guenmai soup—it's only water!"

Nonetheless, guenmai is a practical dish for those who work in the kitchen. If more people come than are expected, then all that is necessary to increase the soup is just to add water to it.

Fuyo Dokai was a great Chinese Master. The Emperor, on hearing about him, invited Dokai to settle in the capital. Dokai refused. Instead he started a Dojo by a lake in the mountains.

Session Three: August 12 – August 20, 1977

And many disciples came to him there. Too many. The Emperor would be jealous. (Dokai was better at getting disciples than I am; he did not do advertising by sticking up posters, and yet still many came.) So Dokai wanted to refuse disciples. This is difficult for a Master to do—to refuse disciples—but some have done it. Bodhidharma did it. (Of course, in modern times there is no such problem. Disciples are always escaping. To make them decide to leave, all I have to do is give them a strong kyosaku.) Anyway, what Master Dokai did was simply never to add guenmai to the soup. He would just add water. The more people came, the more water he added to the soup. So those with big appetites soon left. A good method.

When Professor Okubo Doshu,[36] who is now eighty-five years old, visited the Paris Dojo, he was very impressed with the guenmai soup. Many people had come that day, and Poupoon, the cook, served us only water. He remembers it.

Now I come to the conclusion on how to cut karma. The great Masters have all studied this problem of how to cut bad karma. In particular they have studied the problem of how we think, and so of how we can cut nonmanifest karma. The great Transmitted Masters have all asked themselves these questions. Not just for themselves, but for others. I too think of this. It is the duty, the vocation, the religion of a true monk. So, if you become a monk, you must concentrate upon this problem.

In the end, zazen is the answer.

∼

Many of my disciples are sexually obsessed, and I suffer for them. Those who do lots of zazen become too strong. They smoke (so do I), they drink (so do I), and they have a strong sex drive (I'm

---

[36] Dr. Okubo Doshu: Honorary president of Tokyo and Komazawa Universities. The highest authority on Zen in Japan, and adviser to all the Masters of the Soto Zen sect.

too old for that). I teach my disciples to abandon the ego, and so they quickly abandon their egos. This is a mistake.

Transforming the ego, is that possible?

Because one of the methods for changing our consciousness is through action of body and words (action of the body and of words influences the mind, which in turn influences the body and words), many different Buddhist sects have arisen.

In most Buddhist sects the doctrine of karma is the fundamental column, the fundamental pillar. And so many great monks, wishing to cut their karma, have come to study under all sorts of different Masters.

In Japan today the two principle Buddhist sects are Zen and Nembutsu. Nembutsu, which consists of reciting the name *Namu-Amidabutsu*, is easier than the practice of Zen. Then there is the Obaku sect. Obaku[37] used both Zen and Nembutsu. In the Obaku sect they recite the Nembutsu during zazen. It is very noisy. If you try to concentrate on two or more things at the same time, you get nothing. In the *Shin Jin Mei* it is written that if you concentrate on one thing, you will obtain all things. Those who concentrate on Yoga, Tibetan Buddhism, Karmapa, Rinzai, Soto and the martial arts know nothing of true Zen. But if you concentrate on one, you get all. Shinran, who lived at the same time as Dogen, said that one must concentrate only on Nembutsu. Shinran, in a famous poem, wrote that if we recite the *Namu-Amidabutsu*, all the karma in the three worlds will decrease and finally vanish. Master Daichi wrote that the highest method for cutting bad karma is zazen. Dogen wrote the same thing.

Dogen has written profoundly on this subject of cutting bad karma. He also wrote on the merits of the Kesa. In his *Shobogenzo* it is written that the easiest way to cut karma is to wear the Kesa. For people who cannot do zazen, if they wear the Kesa, they will obtain the great merit required for cutting karma—even

---

[37] *Obaku*: Huang-po in Chinese. Died in 850. A great Master of the Transmission, founder of the Obaku School, and the Master of Rinzai.

Session Three: August 12 – August 20, 1977

nonmanifest karma. It will all vanish. Why? I will explain this another time. Now time is up. Madam has moved her bottom.

Massages this afternoon. And now a mondo.

MONDO

[As is the custom, everyone turns from the wall and faces the Master.]

MASTER: Any questions? No? No questions, then we do zazen again.

QUESTION: Does zazen cut karma?
MASTER: That's my conclusion. You didn't hear me?

QUESTION: Sensei, why is it that the worst kinds of people become monks?
MASTER: Like you?
REPLY: Yes, me. And others.
MASTER: The worst becomes the best. This is Mahayana Buddhism. One's bonnos become the source of Satori. When lots of ice melts, you have lots of water. Big bonnos, transformed by a great Master, will become great Satori. Anyway, what is "worst"? Such standards of good and bad are morals.

QUESTION: When karma is finished, what is left?
MASTER: Satori. Living Nirvana.

QUESTION: Is suffering necessary for the evolution, the progress of man?
MASTER: Yes. But how we solve our suffering is the thing. If you cross through your difficulties, your evolution, your level will change. But if you don't experience difficulty, you cannot progress. This is the problem of modern civilization.

ZEN & KARMA

> Some say that the future civilization will be a spiritual one. The last one was materialistic. But I say that we need both the material and the spiritual. Westerners are always going off to one side. Some Westerners even want to return to prehistoric times.
>
> QUESTION: What is the difference between the Bodhisattva ordination and *Pancha sila*?
> MASTER: Are you Vietnamese?
> REPLY: Yes, Sensei.
> MASTER: They are the same.
>
> QUESTION: Is it possible to practice zazen without the religious ceremonies?
> MASTER: As you like. I educate for my disciples. When my disciples visit Japanese monasteries, they must know how to act. But ceremony is in any case very important. Behaviorism of the body. Sampais too are very effective. And singing the *Hannya Shingyo* decreases your bad karma. No more questions?

Seeking the true religion (Nembutsu, Christianity, Zen…)
Even before Bodhidharma visited China, Nembutsu was widely popular. Nembutsu is a Buddhism of sutras; it is a Tendai, a Jodo, philosophy. Nembutsu practices concentration on the recitation of Amida Buddha's name, and this recitation goes on from morning till night. It signifies: I believe in and respect the Buddha Amida. This name has the same syllable in Hinduism: *nam*.

Amida is not a real Buddha, but rather it is an ideal, like God. And the relationship between Amida and Shakyamuni Buddha in Nembutsu is similar to the relationship between God and Christ found in Christianity. Christianity has had an

Session Three: August 12 – August 20, 1977

influence on Buddhism and Buddhism on Christianity, and it was through Greece that this influence occurred. To better understand this problem, I read books on the subject at the Guimet Museum in Paris.

The two religions, Nembutsu and Christianity, are very similar. The same dualism exists. The dualism found in the relationship which exists between God and man is similar to the dualism found between Amida and man. Similar, too, is the fact that man can go to paradise after death, but that he can never himself become Amida Buddha or God.

When I was young, my mother, who believed very strongly in Amida Buddha, practiced the recitation morning and night. And she made me do the same. I would have to do gassho to Amida Buddha, and then, following my mother, I too would recite his name. But once my mother was in deep concentration, I would escape and only sneak back when it was nearly over. During my student days at the University of Yokohama, I frequented the Christian Church in order to practice my English. The pastor's daughter gave me English conversation lessons, and she also taught me the Bible. This lasted for three years. Anyway, this was when I realized the similarity between Christianity and Amidism. But that is where the similarity ended—the American girl who taught me the Bible and my mother who taught me Amidism were not at all similar. She was twenty-seven or twenty-eight and she was very beautiful, so I left off Amidism and concentrated on Christianity. And on her. She taught me how to dance, too . . .

The only real difference I found between these two religions was in the doctrine of karma. Amidism is deeper than Christianity because of its adherence to the doctrine of karma. Christianity I found to be a bit fatalistic. (I explained earlier the difference between the doctrine of karma and that of fatalism.)

After hearing that the essence of Mahayana Buddhism was to be found in Zen, I went to the Engakuji Temple, a Rinzai Temple, in Kamakura for a sesshin. We got up every morning at 2 a.m. and did zazen until 6 a.m. And at night there was no sleeping. We did zazen outside with the mosquitoes. And then the kyosaku—I received the stick from morning until night, and my body had turned all red. Five days went by. I kept my patience. But then, on the sixth day, the Kyosaku-man, who must have been sleepy like everyone else, hit me with the stick—not on the shoulders, but on top of the head. I got angry and jumped up and hit him back. We fought. Now, in Rinzai Temples, as everyone faces each other while in zazen,[38] they all saw the fight. Everyone jumped up in order to stop me. But I was a champion swordsman at the time, and I had no difficulty keeping them off me. Of course, this has nothing to do with religion; it is just violence. Anyway, I had had enough, and so I went off to see the Master—who was in his room sleeping—and I woke him up and I told him that I wished to leave, that I wanted to stop zazen. I told him all about the incident which had just taken place, and he laughed. "In the history of Zen," the Master said, "no one but you has ever attacked the Kyosaku-man."

In fact, this incident became famous—so much so that Japanese Rinzai monks were scared of me. And my own Master, Kodo Sawaki, would always warn the Kyosaku-man, "Watch out for Deshimaru when you hit him." Consequently, everyone was afraid of me, and so I never got the kyosaku during zazen. The Kyosaku-men always kept clear of me. This is not so good. Later I came to regret that all this had happened.

Sometime after my experience with Rinzai, I went to visit Kodo Sawaki. I told him that I wanted to do zazen. But he said that I shouldn't do it. Too painful. He did not encourage me at all, but instead he suggested I recite the *Namu-Amidabutsu*, because it was easier. I visited Kodo Sawaki again, however—this time at Sojiji Temple. He had me wait for him in his room while he went off to do zazen with his disciples. When he returned, after zazen, he gave me some very strong sake to drink. I had come for zazen, and he wanted to educate me with sake. I was surprised.

---

[38] Not the wall as in Soto.

Session Three: August 12 – August 20, 1977

Anyway, by the time I left I was completely drunk. On my way out, Kodo Sawaki said after me: "You must not let the other monks see you. You must not fall down in the Temple! Fall down outside."

Once outside the gate I sat down under a tree. I sat right down on some dog shit. I got Satori at that moment!

∼

In China, Buddhism developed along two lines—Zen and Nembutsu. (*Nem* means concentration; *Butsu* is the name of Amida Buddha.) In China, up until the time of Mao, until Communism, the temples in Shanghai and in Peking tended to mix the practices of Zen and of Nembutsu. And in Japan, too, this has happened. Soto is the biggest of all the Buddhist sects—Soto has fifteen thousand temples in Japan alone—and next is Nembutsu. Rinzai, Shingon and Tendai are of little importance. Their temples, though, are lovely.

While Zen concentrates upon the doctrine of ku and makes no commentary upon karma, Nembutsu concentrates upon the doctrine of karma and makes no commentary on ku. Dogen himself has never even touched upon this doctrine of karma, while Shinran, the man who spread Nembutsu throughout the whole of Japan, taught only that. He taught that life is nothing but a continuation of karma; and that, as there is no noumenon, life consists of interdependence, of karma.

Until today no transmitted Zen Master has ever touched on this subject of karma. So my kusens here represent a historic teaching. If we can observe and understand our karma, we can more easily understand the meaning of ku. Ku and karma are two different sides of the same coin. We must see both sides. I must explain more, but madam's hips are moving, so time is up.

Mu, when the ego is abandoned
[As is the custom, the Master arrives in the Dojo directly after the others have seated themselves in zazen. A disciple, walking in front of the Master, announces the Master's arrival by striking

the inkin, a little bell he carries in his hand. This ritual takes place at the beginning of every zazen.]

Only one hour, so concentrate on your zazen.

~

I will now continue the kusen on transmigration and samsara.

In ancient Indian thought, transmigration (samsara) was explained in terms of a metaphor as an eternal symbol of human power, of humanity. And Indian Buddhism, since the time of Buddha, has continued to teach transmigration in this manner. So, in India, karma came to be a metaphor for eternity, or for the infinity of Shakti.

In China, however, Chinese realism came to explain transmigration as that of cause and effect. Even after death our mind continues—into eternity. So ever since the development of traditional Indian thought, the motive of transmigration has been cause and effect. All acts performed by people, be they good or bad, become karma, for all acts produce their effects.

On the other hand, if we train our minds and do good, we arrive at *mu* (nothing). And so we become Buddha—and this is the moral significance of transmigration. (Here also we have the relationship between transmigration—reincarnation—and Nirvana.) If, when acting, we break the ten *Kai* (precepts), then certainly we will fall into Naraka (hell). But if we protect and respect the Kai, our faith will change and we will become like the Buddha. We will be reborn in paradise. But if the effects of this good karma come to an end, then we must leave paradise. So, therefore, the absolute state of Nirvana is mu (nothing).

At this moment, human beings can arrive at the state beyond that of transmigration. The state beyond that of transmigration (samsara) is the world of mu.

OPPOSITE: *Ju*—Long life, natural life

寿

So experience mind. Forget, abandon ego. Experience forgetting. Experience the abandoning of the ego. This is the absolute state of mu. Living Nirvana becomes the truth.

"Good causes, good effects": not axiomatic

In ancient Indian Buddhism a contradiction arose over this question of transmigration. Since the Buddhist doctrine of muga denied the reality of the ego, what, then, was being transmigrated? ... So the substance of transmigration was denied. However, later, after the advent of Mahayana Buddhism, the contradiction was embraced. The negative substance of transmigration, along with the doctrine of muga (non-noumenon), was embraced by Mahayana Buddhism.

Mahayana Buddhism explains transmigration in terms of morals—in order that human beings will make an effort in the correct direction. It also explains transmigration in philosophic terms—as a progressing stream, flowing on eternally, in a continued repetition of transmigration. But finally, in the end, Mahayana Buddhism shows that the true Master stands in the highest dimension—beyond attachment to the stream. And this being so, we [the Masters] must not return again to the world of transmigration or reincarnation.

This means living Nirvana—beyond the limits of time. Beyond past, present and future. Here is the absolute state of the world.

So, in Indian Buddhism, the doctrine of karma became similar to that of reincarnation—where cause and effect are perfectly balanced.

In China, Buddhism developed along the lines of good-cause-gives-good-effect and bad-cause-gives-bad-effect; and it worked in well with the moral teachings of Confucius that existed at that time.

All this is complicated. Some people here understand nothing, so they sleep. Yet I am explaining the true essence and the true history of Buddhism—of how it traveled from India to China to Japan, and from Japan to France. And I am explaining karma to you. This is very important. It is also important from the point of view of the history of civilization.

～

[The bell for kinhin has been struck, and everyone gets up.]

At the beginning of the exhalation, step forward about half a foot, and press down hard with the sole of the foot—precisely at the root of the big toe. And then stretch the knee. At this moment the other leg is supple, relaxed.

[The bell ending kinhin has been struck and everyone returns to his or her place.]

Hurry, hurry to your places. Only fifteen minutes more. There is no need to sleep. Some sleep through all the zazens, and when the zazens are over, they are wide awake. Others think that Sensei's kusens are very good. They do not understand their meaning, but they like them anyhow, because they are rhythmic and so it helps them to forget the time.

Manual work rather than manuals

Master Dogen studied Chinese Buddhism, and especially Tendai, near Kyoto. On Mount Hiei. H-U-E-I. Japanese pronunciation is very difficult. So is French pronunciation: Lowwwlllant![39] At first I could not understand R's, H's. In zazen you must not laugh!

Dogen was not satisfied with Tendai Buddhism, so he came down from the mountain and received instruction and education from Eisai, the great Rinzai Master.

Like me: I too first received a Rinzai education from a Rinzai Master in Kamakura. But unlike me, Dogen did not hit the Kyosaku-man. He was a good monk. Besides, at the time when I hit the Kyosaku-man I was not a monk.

Anyway, Dogen was not satisfied with the Rinzai teaching either, so he sailed off to China. Once in China, Dogen visited

---

[39] Laurent: The Tenzo, or Chief Cook, for the Temple.

the Rinzai temples, and other temples too, and he met with many Chinese Buddhist Masters, but he was still not satisfied with the Masters whom he had met, and so he decided to give it all up. He thought then that he had better convert to Catholicism (this is a joke). Anyway, he returned to the harbor to catch the next boat back to Japan.

It was then summertime, and Dogen saw an old monk by the harbor drying out mushrooms in the bright sun. The monk was working like a laborer, but he had a very deep face, and Dogen was impressed. Dogen approached the man and said to him: "I respect you. But why are you busy drying out mushrooms? You are a great monk, and you are old too. Why are you working like this in the hot sun, like a laborer?"

"Because this is my duty. I am the cook for a big temple on Mount Tendo. I am the Chief Tenzo. I am Laurent. And so I must prepare these mushrooms for the Temple. I bought them off a Japanese boat. Japanese mushrooms are of good quality, but these are a bit soggy. It must have been humid on the boat."

"Your temple on Mount Tendo is very far from here," said Dogen. "So let me invite you on board my boat. You can sleep there. And besides, I would like to speak with you."

"No, no. I must return to the temple."

"But why? You need the rest."

"No, no," replied the old monk. "Tomorrow we begin a sesshin, and there are many monks who are counting on me. If I don't return, they won't eat."

"But why did you choose to be the Tenzo?" Dogen persisted. "Why do you prefer to work in a kitchen, when you could be studying books on Buddhism, when you could be studying sutras, when you could become the Chief of a Dojo? Why, instead, have you chosen to be a worker?"

The old monk smiled. "But you are a baby! You know nothing of Buddhism. True Buddhism does not exist in books, nor in the sutras. It exists in practice. Here and now."

This mondo has become very famous in the history of Buddhism. Anyway, Dogen received a very big shock—he has described it in his writing. Dogen got Satori right then! Water—sweat—ran down his back.

"I would like to visit your Temple," Dogen then said.

"I am only the Tenzo. But my Master's name is Nyojo, and he is a great Master. Come, I will introduce you to him."

Dogen visited Master Nyojo after the sesshin. When they met, Dogen was very impressed. Nyojo had a strong face—maybe like mine. And he had big eyes and a big nose. Dogen told Nyojo that he wished to become the Master's disciple.

"Stay here a month or two," answered Nyojo. "You're a cute little Japanese boy."

Dogen was more small than he was tall; at the time he was only twenty-five years old, and he was a good boy. He looked like a gigolo.

Dogen brought true Zen, true true Zen, back to Japan with him. I am omitting the theatrical scene which occurred when Dogen first arrived at the Temple. But I must skip it so that we can finish this sesshin by tomorrow morning.

Dogen forgot all about this problem of karma. He concentrated only on the thought of the beyond, on mu. On transmigration. Muga. On ku. Non-noumenon. This is Shikantaza. Master Nyojo told Dogen that he must spread only true Shikantaza. Dogen had done much deep study on karma, but he was very honest regarding his Master's instructions, and so he followed only Shikantaza.

Behavior influences civilization

There are two ways of educating the human personality. One is the intellectual method—as can be seen with the education of children. "You must do this; you must do that," a mother might say to her child. This method is without practice, but rather is based on intellectual understanding. On knowledge. Such a method is not very effective.

The other way to educate the human personality is by practice. By changing the brain—through morals or, more deeply, through religion. The human must learn to reflect, to be discreet, to restrain himself, to be prudent and moderate, and to have self-control. Think on this question of self-control and you will be able to correct yourself in your daily life.

This second method does not have to do with behaviorism, nor with modern psychology. It has to do with this: Chin in, stretch the backbone, maintain the right posture. This is zazen. Body influences mind. Body does not move during zazen. And so, with an absolutely correct posture—with muscles at the proper tension—your behavior and your posture will influence your thinking.

This is the highest dignity.

There is much thinking going on during zazen, but now it is right thinking, and so now you can see yourselves objectively. And now your thoughts on sex are but shadows passing over a mirror.

In Zen texts you will not find this conception, this analysis, of karma. In Zen, karma is treated as manner, as behavior. And so one's ways in a Dojo are considered very important. When one enters the Dojo, one enters with the left foot, on the left side of the door. One leaves with the right foot, on the right side. In a Dojo it is not only the posture which is important; all the rules are important too. The rules of a Dojo are severe, but one must follow them. Manner educates the spirit, educates the mind.

During the first zazen, in the mornings before breakfast, there are one or two of you who wear your Kesas.[40] You are not to wear the Kesa before breakfast. Only the Chief of the Dojo, the secretary, and those responsible, such as the Kyosaku-man and he who strikes the bell outside the Dojo, can wear their Kesas. No one else. Not even the oldest disciple can wear it. Wearing the Kesa at this time will bring you bad karma. Once the kaijo has been struck, you place your Kesas on top of your heads and chant the *Dai Sai Gedappuku*.[41] Once the chant is over, you put on

---

[40] *Kesas*: Rakusus.
[41] *Dai Sai Gedappuku: Kesa Sutra.*

Session Three: August 12 – August 20, 1977

your Kesas. However, during all other zazens of a sesshin, those who have the Kesa must wear them.

Manner is very important in Zen. Manner is karma. Karma can also mean Kai (the precepts). Follow the precepts and your karma will not go wrong; it will become better. Such an education will bring you to an understanding of muga, of ku (non-noumenon). What is muga? What is ku? My disciples must understand what these mean.

Contrarily, Jodokyo (the Pure Land School) does not talk about muga or ku. One cannot find these concepts within their texts and sutras. The essence of their teaching—of Nembutsu, of the Pure Land School—is karma. The teaching here is that cause and effect are equitably balanced. So in Japan, as I have said, you have two systems, two lines, two columns: Zen and Nembutsu. In Zen, the education is toward substantial humanity. In Nembutsu, it is existential humanity. Both are necessary, and a true Master teaches both. However, in the history of Japanese Buddhism, Zen concentrates purely on substantial personality, Nembutsu on existential personality.

In the end both are the same. Christianity—Catholicism—is similar to Nembutsu, to the Pure Land School. I have experienced them both, and this is what I have found. So, as to this exchange which is occurring between the Oriental and Occidental civilizations, contemporary Christians need not study Nembutsu. But study Zen and you will understand true Mahayana Buddhism. For those who begin, this study is difficult; it is not scientific, and so the study of traditional Zen will be a shock to the Westerners. But as to the exchange between Oriental and Occidental civilizations, a study of Zen is of utmost importance. So if you wish to go beyond the crisis in present-day civilization, then you must study Zen.

The next zazen, this morning at ten, will be the last zazen of this third sesshin.

Training the body-mind

This is the last kyosaku. Everyone should receive it. We must have lots of Kyosaku-men.

[The kusen begins after everyone has received the kyosaku.]

Last kusen. I only hope that you will all continue to practice zazen and Shikantaza. For those who leave today, I hope that next year you will again return to this camp—especially those who have received the Bodhisattva ordinations. Those who have received the Bodhisattva ordination should also try to come to the other sesshins—at Zurich (Switzerland), at Namur (Belgium), in Marseille, Nancy, Wardreque. The sesshins near Marseille and in Zurich are situated in very pretty places. Dokan—the repetition of posture, of body attitude, of manner and of ceremony—is very important. This is not formalism. This is the training of the body.

The Hannya *Shingyo Sutra*—*Shiki soku ze ku, ku soku ze shiki*. We repeat this every day. In the *Shiki soku ze ku, ku soku ze shiki*, you must find the ku in shiki.

In karma you must find ku, the non-noumenon. You must continue zazen in your daily lives. This is ku. In the *Ku soku ze shiki*, you must find the shiki in ku.

In zazen you must observe your karma.

During the *Bussho Kapila Sutra*, which we chant before breakfast, it is said that with the first spoonful we cut all the bad karma. With the second spoonful we create all the good karma. With the third we save humanity . . . This sutra is a long one—especially for beginners. It is very long for just one bowl of guenmai soup.

Observing one's karma

Here you observe yourselves. When you leave, you will forget. *Tant pis*.[42]

During a sesshin it is *Ku soku ze shiki*—if you have observed yourself in your family life, then this sesshin here in Val d'Isére will have great significance for you. Great value.

---

[42] *Tant pis*: Too bad.

Session Three: August 12 – August 20, 1977

So we must understand the meaning of *Ku soku ze shiki, shiki soku ze ku*—that sometimes it is *Ku soku ze shiki*, and sometimes *Shiki soku ze ku*.

In daily life (in shiki) we must find zazen.

In zazen (in muga) we must come to understand our karma.

In daily life (in our karma) we must come to understand our muga, our non-noumenon.

Muga is karma. Muga is *Ku soku ze shiki*. Likewise, karma is muga, non-noumenon: *Shiki soku ze ku*. So muga, zazen and karma are in unity. Nonduality. *Bonno soku Bodai*. *Bonno* is Satori. Zazen is karma. Karma is zazen.

Master Dogen's Zen is not only zazen. It is also to be conscious of all the acts which make up our daily lives. Dogen taught this. Because of this, Soto Zen evolved more in Japan than it did in China or in India. So Zen has penetrated into our daily lives—in the manner of going to the toilet, of cleaning oneself, of conducting one's business, of driving a car—for everywhere Zen exists.

On the other hand, in Japanese Zen one's karma is not observed. And in Christianity karma is ignored. So it is for this reason that I have been talking to you about karma. Japanese Zen Buddhists do not touch upon this subject of karma, and Christian religions do not understand it. So if you have understood the meaning of karma, you can understand the meaning of Mahayana and of Zen. *Shiki soku ze ku, ku soku ze shiki*. Both are necessary.

Interior reflection is very important. Zazen is not simply a sort of gymnastic or a method for obtaining good health. During zazen you must observe your karma. You must reflect on your faults—I do not mean faults in terms of legal or moral laws. Continue zazen, continue to look at your own minds, and so you will understand your faults, and so you will see your deep-rooted bad karma. Reflect deeply upon your sins, your faults, and your objective ego will become Buddha or God. Become Buddha or God and you will have a deep understanding of your karma. "I am the worst of men," and at this moment your objective ego becomes God. Our karma is always in change. Karma is the limit of this world without permanence. One cannot escape karma. It is human thinking. (Or is it the human fault?) This is true zazen. Look objectively at yourselves, look at the substantial ego. Through observation of your karma, you discover how to reflect subjectively.

Madam has not moved her hips today, even though the time has arrived. After zazen we'll have a mondo. Then again zazen. We will be finished by noon.

If you concentrate deeply, even for one day or two days, it will be very effective. If you continue to practice for one year or for ten years, alone in your own home and without concentration, your zazen will be like an open bottle of beer. In zazen it is necessary to always have an élan vital.

MONDO

QUESTION: Could you please explain the duty, the role of the Bodhisattva in modern life?
MASTER: It cannot be limited. If I explain, it will become limited . . . It is not a question of duty, of role. You should see the Bodhisattva in all the different things around you. You must jump into the difficulty. This is hard. This is a Bodhisattva. To help . . . Understand?

QUESTION: Can military men practice zazen?
MASTER: Certainly. Military men are not always killing! Some of them never kill. Prisoners too make good zazen. When I was first a monk in Japan, I used to visit prisoners. I told them that they were the best. Much better than those outside.

QUESTION: Life and death duality—is there harmony beyond life and death in Zen?
MASTER: Yes. This is what I teach. You give a good answer yourself.

Procession after the morning zazen, summercamp at Val d'Isère 1977.

Group photo, summercamp at Val d'Isere 1978.

Chant of the mealtime sutra in the dining hall of
La Gendronniere Zen temple, summercamp 1981.

With his close disciple Etienne Zeisler, see page 72.

With the kyosaku.

With Baker Roshi and Kazuaki Tanahashi, late 1970s.

At a sesshin in St. Baume, France (mid 1970s).

At a reception in California, with Taizen Maezumi (in front, second from the left), Kobun Chino Otogawa (in front, third from the left), Genpo Merzel (3rd row on the right) and other heads of East-coast Zen centers, 1979. Deshimaru's secretary in the 2nd row on the right.

Doing a calligraphy on a rakusu, 1979.

At the party after the summercamp; dressed as a general, 1979.

At a marketplace in Marrakesh, Morocco in 1981.

In the dojo, summercamp Val d'Isère 1977.

With Native American chiefs and with disciples in his apartment in Paris. Philippe Coupey in front on the right. Deshimaru met these chiefs, who were active in the defense of their people and their roots, during his trip to California in 1980.

In Gassho with Alexi Zeisler, 1977, Val d'Isére; see page 50.

Leaving a sesshin with Kodo Sawaki, 1966.

At La Gendronnière, 1980.

OPPOSITE: *Kei sei ei shoku*—If the form is straight, the shadow is straight (Japanese pronunciation: Katachi tadashikereba kage naoshi)

Session Four

August 23 – August 31, 1977

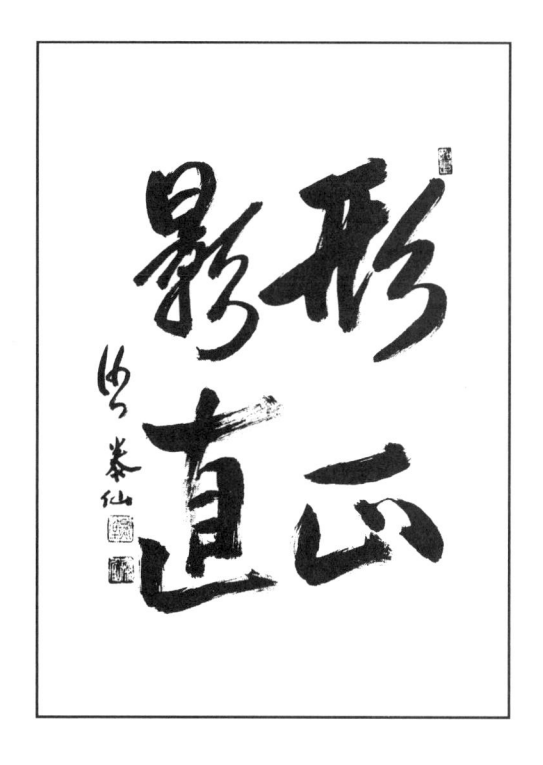

Exact sitting

Today begins the fourth camp, and then the fourth sesshin. The last one. There are about forty or fifty people here who are new to Zen.

What is a sesshin? The kanji *ses* means to touch; *shin* means mind. To touch the mind. To touch the mind of Buddha, of God. What is the mind of Buddha? The fundamental cosmic power. So it means to touch the fundamental cosmic power. It means to follow the cosmic order.

Zazen is complete Shikantaza. Shikantaza means concentration only on zazen. The posture is important. It is not just ordinary sitting. It is nature itself; it is the cosmos itself. Without ego left over. So abandon ego, abandon egoism. You must do zazen with the cosmos. Buddha does zazen. So does God. During zazen you are Buddha, you are God. But during zazen, also, the karma of each of you manifests itself; it arises. Some here want to contemplate, some to observe, some to concentrate. But you must not fix yourselves on any one of these.

If your subconscious arises, your posture will certainly break. So do not hold onto these thoughts. During zazen you must educate all your body, all your mind. You must do this completely. To be devoted to God, or to Buddha, means to follow the cosmic order. If your posture is correct, you can follow the cosmic order. If you are sick, your posture will not be correct, and you will feel pain and sickness. If you have not the habit, and if you have too strong an ego, you will not harmonize with the cosmic order.

For those beginning zazen, please concentrate on your postures. After that, concentrate on your exhalation. Control your breathing. But, in fact, to control your breathing does not mean to control your breathing. Breathing controls itself. Breathing is subjective. Breathing is not done by oneself; it is not done by the consciousness, nor by the ego. Breathing is done unconsciously by the body. It can be said that our breathing, during zazen, is the action of nature, of the cosmos. So the reason for this breathing is its rhythm. It is the rhythm of the fundamental cosmic power.

Chin in! Chin in!

As much as possible, stretch your backbones—especially from the waist. And when you move, you must do gassho first. If you do not follow the rules, the Kyosaku-man will give you the kyosaku.

～

During zazen, surely your bonnos—your karma—will arise. Like waves on the sea. Some people have big waves, some quiet waves. The size of the waves depends upon one's health. The waves arrive—and some of you are like in a storm. Then the waves come back to normal, and the surface of the water becomes like a mirror. But to come back to normal is very difficult. Everybody has karma. And when the winds of karma blow, the waves grow. But continue this sesshin and possibly you will return to the normal condition, and the surface of the water will then become like a mirror. Anyway, if your posture is correct, so also your breathing will be correct; it will harmonize with the cosmos. Dogen said: "Right body, right posture, straight sitting—this is what controls the breathing."

We must not satisfy our egoistic tendencies, nor must we seek personal satisfaction. If you imagine a certain satisfaction during zazen, then you have an object to satisfy. However, during zazen it is not possible to run after effects, after results.

After half an hour of zazen, we do kinhin. No doubt the educators, in your preparation period before this zazen, have explained to you the true method of zazen and of kinhin. Kinhin is the same as zazen. Mind is the same. It is walking zazen. When you hear the two bells which announce kinhin, first you do gassho. Then you place your hands, thumbs enclosed in their fists, on your knees, and you swing back and forth, with larger and larger swings, seven or eight times. Next you give a big breath, a big exhalation, and pressing your fists on the ground, you stand up. If you cannot uncross your legs, rub them with your hands. After that, get up calmly, turn to the right around

Session Four: August 23 – August 31, 1977

your zafu, do gassho to the zafu,[43] and push your zafu back into shape. If you are in pain, stretch your knees as you push down on your zafus. Then you arrange your zafu against the wall, and you do kinhin.

∽

[The bell for kinhin has been struck and everyone gets up and begins kinhin.]

During kinhin the eyes are very important. You must concentrate them three meters in front of you on the lower back of the person in front of you. During kinhin you must not look at the faces of others.

[The bell ending kinhin has been struck and everyone returns to his or her place.]

∽

A sesshin is absolutely necessary

Zazen is the complete opposite of dancing. Dancing is entirely the phenomenon of our karma. Man wants to move. In ancient times man was obliged to move for his work. He traveled on foot to find food. He went without car, without train. From morning to evening he was always moving, moving. But in modern civilization man does not move so much. So he moves instinctively at night—he dances. The intellectuals too dance. And when these intellectuals dance, their heads, which are too heavy, move about the most. I saw this at the Santa Lucia[44] when I went there. Karma is rising, like fire.

When a man dances, he feels nothing; he doesn't even feel it when someone touches him. In zazen, however, you can feel

---

[43] The gesture of salutation is directed not to the zafu, but to those who have been sitting nearby in zazen.

[44] The local Val d'Isére nightclub.

everything—the sounds of nature, the sound of the river of Val d'Isére.

In ancient times man could return to nature; he could return to the cosmos. Modern man, however, has forgotten how to return; he has forgotten how to harmonize with nature. In fact, modern man is no longer able to follow the cosmic order. So zazen is absolutely necessary. A sesshin is absolutely necessary. You must follow the cosmic order. Abandon ego. Then you will be able to follow it automatically, naturally, unconsciously. And so you will find the fundamental cosmic power.

Beginning people are very fresh. But the permanents, here in their fifth week, are not so fresh. During their free time they go dancing. With too much nighttime dancing they are no longer able to follow the time schedule. They can no longer follow Dokan. This morning, those responsible for the wake-up bell forgot to ring it. And so everybody stayed sleeping in their beds. Except me; I was the first up. So I had to ring the bell. The permanents here, who stay for all four camps, must be an example for the new people. But, as it is, most of the responsible people deserve a strong rensaku. I should give the rensaku myself to all my disciples. But there are too many of them, and it would only tire me out. So please reflect—just to the end of this sesshin. To those who cannot reflect I will give the rensaku.

[Someone has fallen ill and is being helped out by the Kyosaku-man.]

Some of the beginning people find this atmosphere here too severe—those who are weak and those who are sick. Those whose bodies and minds are not in the normal condition surely receive a big shock, because Shikantaza is very powerful. Those whose egos are too strong cannot go into the cosmos, and so they fall down.

Karma repeats itself
Up through the third sesshin I talked of karma. When you steal once, the karma created soon repeats itself and you steal again, two times, three times and so on. The first time the theft is not so

Session Four: August 23 – August 31, 1977

big, and no one even notices it. But then it gets bigger and bigger, and you go to prison, and when you are free again you kill someone. This is the manifestation of karma. How do you cut it?

During this camp, someone here, someone who does zazen, has been stealing. Three times now this person has stolen. I know who has been doing it, too. I know exactly—by intuition. He is not one of the new people; he is one of the permanents. But, as no one knows who it is but me, I will not mention his name. I will keep the name for myself, because I respect him. However, again today a hundred and fifty francs were stolen. Not from the same room as the last time, but from the room opposite. He goes into rooms and steals. Not big sums. A hundred francs here, two hundred there. During the last sesshin he stole two hundred francs from behind the bar. And it is always done by the same person. He always steals at the same time—when a sesshin is over and the people are leaving. It is childish. He has until tomorrow night to confess. If he does not confess, I will order him out. But if he confesses, it will remain a secret—I will not tell others who he is. I will give him protection. If necessary, I will give him money. If he confesses, his karma will be finished. And later he will be able to cut it.

I know who it is by intuition. I know by looking at the person from behind, by looking at his posture during zazen. It is not good to steal during a sesshin, during zazen. This is the worst. If you do it at the Club Méditerrané or at the Santa Lucia—*tant pis*. But this is not a hotel. This is a holy place! A saintly place!

So he can come to me tomorrow evening during zazen. He can come between four and five o'clock. He can come to my room—I will be there. Please. So that I can kiss him. So that I can give him money.[45]

---

[45] By three o'clock the Master grew impatient, and so, instead of waiting in his room until four o'clock, he went himself to the thief's room. The thief confessed; and at the same time he asked if he could be ordained a Bodhisattva. The Master, of course, was happy and granted the man his wish.

A tree knows neither happiness nor unhappiness

This morning I talked about the zazen posture itself being God or Buddha. And that it was also nature and the cosmos itself. Man is of the same existence as the sun or the stars in the cosmos. It is the same—the man who catches a cold and the black spots which appear on the sun. Man is the same—like mushrooms on the surface of the earth.

Zazen is the fact of nature; it is beyond the human being.

During zazen voluntary action is forbidden. Rinzai Zen, which has you work on koans during zazen, is completely wrong on this issue. Koans are like games, intellectual games. It is not real zazen. Certainly it is interesting to think: "What is mu?" "What were my thoughts before I was born?" But this is impossible to solve. You can never solve a koan. "What is tonton?"[46] The ideogram tonton in Japanese means pork. So when a disciple answers by saying that tonton is uncle, the Master says, "No, no, no. Tonton is pork!"

In this world, intellectuals run after mistaken truths—mistaken truths which they alone understand. The intellectual creates a category which he then says is the truth. But this is his own personal truth. He has created it by himself. He has an image, and he says: "This is the truth. This is Satori. Satori is like this." This is *his* Satori. This is tonton Satori. But it is not the truth. We must not imagine Satori. Such people are merely running after their own satisfactions, after their own personal desires. It is the same as running after sex or beefsteak.

So a man who finds his own Satori, all by himself, is only finding self-satisfaction. Auto-satisfaction must not be practiced during zazen. One must abandon this completely, and so harmonize with the cosmic order. This is true zazen.

In man there are accidents; in the cosmos there are—none. In man there is success or failure; in nature, in the cosmos, there is not—no success, no failure, no happiness, no unhappiness. In

---

[46] *Tonton*: A colloquial French word for uncle.

man there is the good and the bad, but in nature there is neither. It is man himself who has made these categories of good and bad, success and failure, happiness and unhappiness. But once one is in unity with the cosmos, then there is no success and no failure. With mountains, rivers, plants and trees there is no success, no failure. When man cuts down a tree, even then the tree does not become sad. The tree knows no happiness or unhappiness. It simply follows the cosmic order. People believe that it is right to hate the bad. But it is to hate, this is what is bad. Mountains, rivers, flowers, trees do not hate. They have no mind from which to hate. In the cosmos there is nothing miraculous, nothing strange, nothing bizarre. But man does not know the cosmos. He ignores it. So therefore he finds things miraculous, strange and bizarre.

Right posture influences everyone else

Don't move. Don't move. Those who wish to move must first do gassho. The movers should sit in the back row so as not to disturb the others. Or sit outside. Many here are always scratching—like monkeys. Or else they are giving themselves massages. It is up to the Kyosaku-man to correct postures, and to give the kyosaku to those who move without first doing gassho.

This Kyosaku-man must be crazy—he corrects the wrong people! [To the other Kyosaku-man:] Give the person in white the rensaku. Ten times on each shoulder. People who receive the rensaku must reflect: Why have I received the rensaku?

During my long experience in zazen, I have noticed that those who sit near the person receiving the kyosaku move. So the Kyosaku-man must not precipitate giving the kyosaku. The kyosaku is most effective for those who do not want it. But it is most important to give the kyosaku to those who move all the time.

Pas bouger![47] The Kyosaku-man must look, must observe. See who moves, who disturbs. The Kyosaku-man is not a

---

[47] *Pas bouger:* Don't move.

marionette. Nor is he a dog-killer. He must sense those whose minds move. He must observe the mind. Those who practice zazen are not dogs.

Chin in. Stretch the backbone. These are the two most important points in posture. Some lean to the left, some to the right. Some have their shoulders up, others down. They are not in balance. For those who have too much tension, the Kyosaku-man must press down on their shoulders with his hands.

The two states kontin and sanran are both bad. One is too mushy, the other too excited. In kontin the mind is down and dark, dark. The chin falls, the thumbs fall, the backbone bends. This is kontin. Sanran, which is the opposite, means that you are in too much tension. Those in sanran move their eyes and look at the others. Their heads move; their hands move. There is too much tension in their shoulders. All this must be corrected. But if correction does not work, then the Kyosaku-man must give the kyosaku.

Those here who fall into one of these two states and who cannot correct themselves by themselves must ask for the kyosaku. Asking for the kyosaku is not just something in fashion, something you ask for just because your neighbor asks for it. Nor is it to be asked for out of diplomacy.

A person with the right posture influences all the others, all the cosmos. A person with the wrong posture also influences all the others, all the cosmos.

Without fear, free
Freedom, what is freedom? I don't know. Is it freedom to follow one's ego, one's desires? It is to follow the cosmic order. This is a great koan.

When we are afraid of death, we are not free. But follow the cosmic order and there is no need to be afraid of death. When we are free from the fear of death, we are completely free. Our lives are but foam on the stream of cosmic consciousness.

There is no need to commit suicide. This is weakness. We must live for eternity.

Session Four: August 23 – August 31, 1977

∼

[The Master addresses one of the Kyosaku-men:] Kyosaku-man, you must stop giving the kyosaku. You are not a strong Kyosaku-man. You are not at all effective. Better that you stand still, like a mannequin.

After the bell no one must move. You must not yawn either. But if you do, then put your hand over your mouth first. When you yawn in zazen it means that you are too tense.

When you are about to begin zazen, first swing back and forth seven or eight times, exhale and inhale deeply, and then slowly, slowly let your breathing flow calmly in and out.

[The Master addresses one of the monks:] Alain—you must give the kyosaku. Help the Kyosaku-men. [The monk, following the custom, removes the kyosaku from the altar below the Buddha statue and joins the other Kyosaku-men.]

During the kusen, if the Kyosaku-man sees that it is necessary to give someone the kyosaku, then he can do so. But he must not give it to those who ask. The initiative must come from the Kyosaku-man.

∼

[The Master addresses one of the monks sitting in zazen:] Michel! You are the *Godo*[48] here. Help the Kyosaku-man.

In a true Dojo, the *Godo* is the educator of the disciples. The Godo is the most important position after the Chief of the Temple. The Godo sits to the left of the rear entrance and directly in front of the Chief (who sits at the other end of the Dojo and to the right of the front entrance). The Godo must observe the others in their zazens, and in their daily lives—in the

---

[48] *Godo*: *Go* means behind, rear, back; *do* means hall, Dojo. Thus, strictly speaking, Godo means the rear of the Dojo. In the larger sense, the Godo is he who educates the disciples.

lives of each one of them—so that he will know to whom he should give the kyosaku. We are not at the Club Méditerrané.

[To one of the Kyosaku-men:] No good kyosaku! You must stop. Just stand.

If the Kyosaku-man makes mistakes, this is not at all good, because his mistakes influence. Those who receive the kyosaku from a Kyosaku-man who makes mistakes will also make mistakes in Zen.

Don't move. Don't move.

Neither strange nor miraculous
In Zen the most important thing is to concentrate here and now. During zazen, during the kusen, concentrate on Shikantaza, concentrate on the kusen. When you get out of your bath, the kusens are not so important; it is more important, at this point, to put on clean underwear. When you wake up in the morning, the kusens are not so important either; it is more important that you put on your pants first... And now, on what must we concentrate? If we concentrate here and now, if we concentrate on this point, our concentration will become like a connected geometric line, and so our lives will thus become concentrated. But if the here-and-now is empty, our lives too will be empty; and when finally we enter the coffin—alone—the coffin too will be empty.

∽

At the beginning of the *Shin Jin Mei*, a poem by Master Sosan, the Third Patriarch after Bodhidharma, it is written that the highest way is not difficult—only we must not select. We must avoid selection.

What is good? What is bad? People like to say that to hate the bad is good. But actually it is the mind, or the spirit, of hate which is bad. Mountains, trees, rivers have no mind with which to hate. I have always said that in the cosmos there are no miracles, no mysteries, no nothing. But as man does not know the cosmos, he sees miracles.

Session Four: August 23 – August 31, 1977

My Master, Kodo Sawaki, always repeated Master Daichi's words: If we want to cut life and death, if we want to cut the impermanence of life and death, Shikantaza is the best method, it is the highest way.

Zazen is the practice of sitting facing the wall, quietly, without causing movement with the body, without speaking with the mouth, without thinking good or bad with the consciousness; it is to sit peacefully on a zafu in some quiet place. Zazen is only this. Shikantaza. There is nothing strange in this, nothing miraculous. And there are no special particular reasons for it. However, the merit from Shikantaza is infinite. So please do not pass the time in an empty way; do not pass the time vainly.

Now I will sing you the *Fukanzazengi*. In Japanese temples in the evenings we always sing the *Fukanzazengi* together. But as you do not know it, I will sing it alone. The *Fukanzazengi*, written by Master Dogen in the year 1233, consists of the general rules concerning the practice of zazen.

Concentrate only on your zazen. We need not concentrate on anything else.

A physical education

Some people are always picking their noses during zazen. And then they play with the snot. You can do that after zazen. Or first do gassho, and then use a handkerchief. But don't poke in your noses with your fingers. The Kyosaku-man must watch for these things. He is not just to give the kyosaku. He must educate as well. And see that the chins are in, that the tension in the backbone is correct.

Those who are in pain, and who are always moving, correct yourselves at the level of your zafus. The zafu is maybe to one side or the other. Your hips must be situated over the center of the zafu, with your bottom a little to the front. Push down on the zafu with the coccyx, but not with the anus. The anus must point upward.

"Not possible," think the disciples.

"Possible by mind," [replies the Master].

The coccyx, a small bone located at the lower end of the vertebrae and around the sexual organs, is a point of acupuncture, and it is a very important point—a point of energy. So if you push down on this point on your zafu, it is very effective and excellent for the health. It is like an auto-massage lasting for an hour.[49] But if your waist sags, then it is not at all effective. So you must stretch the waist. [To the Kyosaku-man:] The method for correcting a sagging waist is to give punches in the area of the back—in the hollow of the back—which should go in. Sometimes I poke this point with the end of the kyosaku.

During the kusen, one's manner of sitting is very important. The posture, breathing, attitude of mind, this is called *Kuden*—transmission by the mouth, secretly, from Master to disciple.

Complete communion

In Christianity, praying to God is very important. In Zen, there is the word *Kito*. Kito means grace, it means ceremony; but it does not mean prayer to God. During sesshins I too do a little Kito. During the chanting of the *Hannya Shingyo*,[50] I open the big sutra book, the mystical sutra called the *Rishu Kyo*.[51] I open it and manipulate it back and forth like a fan. But this is not for God, nor for the Buddha. It is for man—for his personal good health, etc. It is a ceremony of low dimension, and not of the essence. It is the phenomenal side to the *Hannya Kyo*.[52]

---

[49] Until the zazen is over.
[50] *Hannya Shingyo*: Hannya means the highest wisdom—*Prajna* in Sanskrit. *Shin* means essential faith, the essence. *Gyo* (or *Kyo*) means sutra. See Glossary.
[51] *Rishu Kyo*: Sutra in praise of Sex, in praise of the original instinct in man. The *Rishu Kyo* is the phenomenal side—the other side from the *Hannya Kyo (Gyo)*.
[52] *Hannya Kyo*: Wisdom Sutra.

Session Four: August 23 – August 31, 1977

When I was young, I always wondered why God never answered our prayers. I even asked a priest this question: "Why does God not answer prayers?"

"God's answer is silence," replied the priest.

I was impressed. This priest was very clever. But clever or not, this is not an answer; later I realized this. Saint Augustine has said that prayer is a conversation with God. So if it is a conversation, then it is not silence—an answer is necessary. In Zen mondos, a Master's answers can sometimes be silence—yet this in itself is a personal answer. The Master is silent, but afterwards he gives an answer. With God, though, this is not so.

In the end God does answer one's prayers. And at this time we have what is called Communion, as you know. The Trinity: The Father, the Son and the Holy Spirit. In the end we communicate with the Trinity. We have total Communion with God, or with Christ. However, this is merit, this is the effect of prayer. But this is not an answer. This is simply merit, effect.

Meister Eckhart—he was a famous Dominican, wasn't he? You know more about him than I do. Anyway, he was a German philosopher, and he wrote many books. He lived from 1260 to 1329—about the same time as Dogen. Eckhart had a mystical experience. Eckhart said that if you pray to God, if you ask for God, God will answer you thus: "You are My Son." This is the most intimate answer from God, and it is the birth which produces this filiation. So God in heaven answers His Son. In the answer, the Holy Mind enters into the Son, and at this moment we have Communion.

But in Zen, through the practice of zazen, through the body, we can communicate directly with the fundamental cosmic power. This approach is more rational, more scientific, and not at all mysterious. It is beyond the scientific. So do zazen and you can become the Son. This is not complicated.

In European philosophies, and in their religions, the body has been neglected. The body has been regarded as unimportant. The spirit alone is important. This is so with religions in general. Too much spirituality. Too much imagination of the brain. And so we have the imaginative, the mysterious. And so we have miracles. Miracles come from ignorance. In the cosmic order there are no miracles.

And so now we have the Pope. The Pope wants to use zazen. He has ordered me to join him in Italy in September—to go from monastery to monastery, to give conferences, and to educate the Christian monks in zazen. All this is very clever.

Do not neglect the body
Zazen itself, the posture itself, is God, is Buddha. Zazen itself is the Son. It is not necessary to construct complicated philosophies over this. Christ himself and his teachings were, I think, not so complicated. Rather, they were very simple. Only later did they become complicated. Philosophy became complicated. Theology became complicated.

Theology merely plays with ideals; it is imagination without practice. It is time and energy wasted.

∼

Kinhin!

[Everyone rises, arranges his or her zafu against the wall and begins kinhin.]

Stretch the neck, stretch the knees. Almost everyone here now has a good posture. Very dignified. Better than Buddha, better than God.

[The bell ending kinhin has sounded and all return to their places.]

Hurry, hurry. Those by the window are always the last to sit down. Three Kyosaku-men are needed. Michel, you take the kyosaku. You must educate the others.

Don't move; after the bell you are not to move. Some people here are always moving their heads—like toy dogs.

Stretch the neck. This is very important. Chin in.

∼

Session Four: August 23 – August 31, 1977

The mystical experience in Christianity is different from the zazen experience. The mystical experience is imaginative. It separates mind and body. The body is dirty, and so the mind, which wants to become pure, escapes from the body. And with a pure mind, Communion, unity, can come about between God, the Holy Spirit, and the Son. This is imagination. Neglect the body and it all becomes a dream. A dream. And so religions have become weak.

Zazen is the opposite. Posture—it is posture which brings us back to reality. Chin in. Push down on the zafu with the sexual organs; push the sky with the head. This way we can communicate unconsciously, automatically and naturally with God, with the fundamental cosmic power.

The Rinzai Masters of modern times like to make comparisons between Zen and the mystical experiences of Eckhart. Eckhart is very close to Zen. He has written that one should abandon the ego. And in Rinzai Kensho it is said that you must find Buddha's nature—Kensho, the true ego—in your own mind. This is very close to Catholicism. Rinzai and Catholicism thus understand each other quite well. Rinzai and Soto Zen, however, are not the same. In Soto Zen there is Mushotoku—nothing. There must be no object during zazen. Just concentrate on the posture. This is very difficult for the body.

When we pray to God, when we are in the act of prayer, a posture is necessary. What is our posture when we pray to God? How, at this time, do we breathe? And what, at this time, do we do with our consciousness? Now it becomes complicated.

Neoplatonism, which influenced Eckhart, neglected the body. And from this thought, from this attitude, mysticism arose. Through prayer to God, the mystic escapes the body to enter into the world of the soul—where he can then communicate with God, with absolute existence.

Though Eckhart was influenced by the mystical Neoplatonists, he did not particularly neglect the body. And, contrary to Descartes, Eckhart denied that the soul escapes from the body. No duality exists between body and mind in Eckhart's philosophy.

One must be beyond duality, beyond opposition of body and mind, Eckhart wrote. All existences are in unity. And he goes on to explain about universal love, which, he says, is without profit. This is close to Zen. This is similar to Mushotoku.

I will continue tomorrow.

God has no need of conversation
The highest posture of prayer to God is zazen. In Christianity, prayer to God is conversation with God. When we here wish to talk with God, we take the posture of gassho. And so we hope, we wish, for something. But this has a goal. It is not Mushotoku.

In zazen we are not in gassho—our hands are in the position of Hokai join. The hands, during zazen, are situated under the navel and in front of the kikai-tanden. The cosmos enters into the kikai-tanden, and we have complete communication with the fundamental cosmic power.

For God, conversation is not necessary. Nor is it necessary for you. It is not necessary for you to ask Him for anything. There is no duality between God and man. When in harmony with the cosmic order, man becomes God.

In zazen we do not pray; we do not ask anything of God. Zazen itself becomes God. This is the absolute silent conversation during zazen.

Eckhart has said that God's answer, during prayer, is the product of the Son. A little complicated, this answer. During zazen, God and zazen are in unity—this is God's answer when we are in zazen. God penetrates into zazen. Hokai join—it is the same thing.

The effect of zazen is infinite—infinite merit. The merit of God must be infinite. If it is limited, then it is not God.

When consciousness becomes physical
During zazen I always say Mushotoku. Mushotoku-mind. There is nothing to obtain; during zazen there is no goal. If there is, if you have a goal, then you are making a big mistake. Zazen means to stop everything, to abandon everything—even one's philosophy.

Session Four: August 23 – August 31, 1977

Someone here—a doctor—has just escaped the sesshin. He got up during the middle of zazen and said: "I can't get anything from Zen!" Then he walked out.

This man has certified true Mushotoku: that there is nothing to get from Zen. If you do get something, then it is not true Zen, not true Soto Zen.

In primitive India, after the Buddha's time, one of the schools of Buddhism did an analysis of Zen, decomposing it into four steps or stages. These steps were merely steps toward obtaining Satori. But they are not necessary. It is not necessary to make steps. Bodhidharma and Dogen did not use steps. The zazen of a beginning person and the zazen of someone who has practiced it for a long time are the same, for to do zazen is itself Satori.

However, for beginning people these four steps exist. But during zazen we must not think of such things. "I am in the second stage . . . Now I am in the third." And with big smiles on our faces—like mad people. "I have abandoned all, and now I am in the final stage. Certainly I have gotten Satori." Not true.

I am always saying "automatically, naturally, unconsciously." We must concentrate only on posture. Then we can attain the Holy Spirit, the body spirit—automatically, naturally, unconsciously.

Most people here are in the first stage. All they want is pleasure. After some painful zazens, they are quick to run off to the Santa Lucia and buy whiskey. Getting Satori, they rush onto the dance floor and begin to move.

Anyway, our minds grow peaceful and true pleasure comes. This is the first stage. It is like ecstasy.

In the second stage, our will, our consciousness, our prudence disappear, and we are penetrated with joy right down to the bottom of our bodies. We are Mushotoku. But still we dream of going dancing at the Santa Lucia.

In the third stage, our mind is absorbed into the body. The tired neurons of the brain are no longer tired, and the brain becomes completely pure. Thinking and imagination have been abandoned, and all necessary thinking occurs through intuition.

(As for myself, I do not think. Not at all. This way, new thoughts are always arising. I do not want to think by myself—but thoughts come anyhow, and so wisdom arises. Automatically, unconsciously, naturally.)

In the fourth stage, it is no longer necessary to be happy. Happiness is not true purity. At this stage we abandon attachment, we abandon everything, and so there is only purity. This is true Mushotoku. This is Satori.

Stages?

When, during zazen, thinking stops, mind becomes body. This is an important point. Yet most people—the philosopher, the intellectual, and the adolescent—believe the opposite, that body becomes mind. These sorts of people, and especially the young today, in seeking their pleasure, satisfaction and enjoyment, absorb it into their brains via the body. So body becomes mind. On the dance floor, when taking drugs, drinking whiskey, or having sex, our experiences are through the body. This is contemporary civilization. Danceology, drugology, philosophy, psychology—they are all like this. But in true religion, and especially in zazen, it is the opposite.

If we continue zazen, in the end we can attain true freedom of mind. True freedom right down to the bottom of our minds. True freedom not attained by anything from the exterior . . . When Christ prayed to God from morning until night, he found the Holy Spirit—in his mind. He found the highest contentment, the highest pleasure. It was beyond pleasure. It was without Mushotoku. Without anything. The mind becomes completely absorbed into the body. Thinking is finished, and only cosmic thinking penetrates the body.

The Holy Spirit entered into Christ's mind. And there was only the world of God . . . Likewise during zazen: When we hear the sound of the valley of Val d'Isére, the sound penetrates the body completely, and there is only the sound of the valley. Mind is nothing. The sound is that of the voice of God. The green of the mountains becomes the pure mind of God, the pure mind of

Session Four: August 23 – August 31, 1977

Buddha. True religion does not have to do with imagination, nor with brain-thinking.

In October I must go to Italy. I am to go from monastery to monastery, and when this is over, I am to join the Pope at the Vatican. So now I am preparing for this visit.

～

Experience through the body is very important. It is with the body that we pray to God. Protestant or Catholic, meditation without prayer to God with the body is not valid. What is our posture when we pray to God? And what was Christ's? What was his posture? His breathing? How was his consciousness? How was his thinking?

Christ too abandoned everything in the end. He was without attachment. In the end, he had no object vis-a-vis God. All imagination, all philosophy, all the products of thinking, all communication with God were absorbed into Christ's body, absorbed into the body's very depths. In the end, it was the fundamental cosmic power which filled Christ's body. It was the Holy Spirit.

The Holy Spirit is not created, nor does it begin, nor is it produced from our minds. When our mind is empty the Holy Spirit enters, the fundamental cosmic power enters. From mind to body. Mind to body.

Of course, if we believe that all the cosmos is God, if we believe that all the cosmos is the illumination of Buddha—if this is our faith, then this faith will grow deeper, deeper, and it [this light of God, this illumination of Buddha] will penetrate down to the bottom of our bodies, down to the bottom of our minds. Through the practice of zazen, this cosmic energy which spreads throughout the worlds will penetrate our entire personality. The light of God, the illumination of the Buddha which penetrates throughout our bodies and minds, fills the entire cosmos infinitely, eternally.

This mutual interdependence existing between the fundamental cosmic power and myself, between God and myself, grows bigger, grows larger, grows deeper; and so our religious life must be more and more cultivated.

ZEN & KARMA

The Way, the Truth, Christianity, Buddhism—all religions are in the end the same. I think so. Climb a mountain, and from its top you can see the Way, the Truth; you can see all the Ways; you can see life.

I am the Way; I am the Truth; I am life.

MONDO

We have questions now for those who wish to obtain something. New people here who want to get something, come closer.

QUESTION: Sensei, you mentioned the four stages. Does a person fluctuate through these stages, or not? If, for example, a person is in stage three, does he remain fixed there, or does he—can he—go up to four or maybe drop to one?

MASTER: Of course. This is not like an elevator!

In Zen many classifications have arisen around these stages. There is *Naraka Zen*, which is the most famous. When you are in pain, you are in *Naraka*.[53] Like beginning people. Like the doctor who left today. He was surely in Naraka. I shook hands with him when he left. I gave him a calligraphy and told him to continue zazen. He was very happy, but nevertheless he was in Naraka.

After Naraka Zen you have *Kaki Zen*. A man in Kaki Zen is a man who avidly searches for something. [The Master does a caricature of an avid man.] Kaki means appetite, avidity. A man in such a state is always trying to get something, even from Zen. Like the doctor: When he realized that he was not going to get something, he stood up in the middle of zazen and walked out.

---

[53] *Naraka*: Hell.

Then you have *Animal Zen*. A man in this stage always thinks of sex. He stares at the buttocks of the woman in front of him. [The Master does a caricature.]

A boy once said to me: "Whenever I sit next to a female, I feel my sex organ. And sometimes I've even ejaculated. All this is very difficult for me. How can I stop it?"

"Very easy," I replied. "Just don't sit next to women."

Asura Zen is competition Zen. [The Master does a caricature.] "I am better. My posture is perfect!" Even during mealtime, the man in Asura thinks this way: "I must sit at the table with the golden disciples."[54] And in the Dojo it is the same. One woman in particular is always pushing others so that she can get closer to Sensei. She pushes Philippe, she pushes Anne-Marie, and she pushes me—right out the door.

In the *Zen of Ecstasy*, one's zazens are quiet, one's mind is peaceful, joyous. A man in this stage never asks for the kyosaku, and sometimes he is smiling. [The Master does a preposterous caricature.] Or crying. This is especially so with women. I see them. It is their subconscious arising.

You also have the *Dogmatic Stage*. "I got Satori. Exactly Satori!" [The Master does another caricature.] "I got Satori. The others are crazy." Bodhisattvas are not so.

In the end you have *Personal Zen*. This is the Zen of man.

The tenth step is that of Bodhisattvas and Buddhas. It is called the *Shobogengaku*.

The first six stages are not so good. The following four are the stages of the sage—of ordinary men and of wise men.

There exist many kinds of classifications. The Bodhisattva and the Buddha stages represent the return to the normal condition. Completely normal.

---

[54] The Master's principal disciples.

ZEN & KARMA

QUESTION: My question was: Is there change in the individual from one stage to the next?
MASTER: You do not experience this yourself? Even me, I experience this. When I want to go make *pipi* during zazen, I sit on my pipe and try to be patient. This is Naraka. Buddha himself, when he was doing zazen under the Bodhi tree, experienced Naraka in the form of women. He saw [in his hallucination] many beautiful women come to him and torment him. It is from this experience of the Buddha's that we have the *Kegon Sutra*. The Kegon Sutra is very interesting—it expresses all the conditions of zazen.

Every day is different. Every instant is different. When zazen begins we are in good shape; next we are in pain; then in ecstasy.

Me, too—I've not progressed in zazen at all. I've gotten worse. In the beginning I was the best. In the beginning I was completely concentrated, I had forgotten everything, and my zazens were utterly pure. But nowadays I am much more clever. Now, during zazen, even when I sleep I don't fall over like I did before. Once when I did a forty-day sesshin—without sleep, not even at night—we would use a special stick with a rounded end—like this one—to support our chins. But now I am much more clever, and when I sleep not even Anne-Marie, who sits next to me, notices it. The only difference, when I sleep, is that there is no kyosaku, no kusens. But you must not imagine that just because there are no kusens, Sensei is sleeping. Nor must you be anxious about my forgetting the time. When it comes to the hour, I am very exact. Anyway, it is not good to sleep during zazen.

Everybody goes through many different stages. Still, you must never forget your beginning zazens, your beginning times—Dogen said this. In the beginning you are completely concentrated. In the beginning you forget everything. And when this is so, you are practicing the true zazen of Satori.

Once I had a big problem: I had to go *pipi*, and to block my pipes I pushed down hard on them. This is when I experienced Rinzai Kensho—I fell into a coma. This is Rinzai Satori, to fall into a coma.

When Rinzai was still a disciple, he went to see Master Obaku one day for a mondo—which has since become famous—and he asked Obaku what was the essence of Zen. The Master hit his disciple very hard with the kyosaku. Rinzai returned to his own room, and there he found several old disciples waiting for him.

"Why have you come back?" one of them asked. "You must return and ask your question again."

So Rinzai returned, repeated the question, and received fifty more blows with the kyosaku. It was simply a football game.

In modern times it is the same—lots of theater. The zazens go on for one, two, three weeks without sufficient food. And so your consciousness becomes psychological. Your brain becomes weak and abnormal, and at this time you can fall into a coma. In this state of consciousness—which is not the normal state—you experience many bonnos, many phenomena; you see Buddha and the demons. And in the end you forget your body, and you are in complete paradise. "You now have Satori," the Master says at this time. But this is not Satori. This is merely a psychological sickness, a Zen sickness.

In true, true Zen you are woken up by something. When crossing through many difficulties, if you remain patient, your mind sometimes changes.

Dogen too once received a big shock. Master Nyojo was very angry with the monk sitting next to Dogen—the monk was sleeping—and Nyojo hit him hard and shouted in a loud voice: "*Shin jin datsu raku!*"[55] Dogen, who had never had such an experience, was shaken, shocked and surprised. Dogen, at this moment, had Satori.

Dogen did not get Satori. Dogen did not want Satori. What occurred was a complete metamorphosis of Dogen's body and mind. A big revolution. So after zazen Dogen paid the Master a visit in his room. He did sampai. "Today I have completely understood. Body and mind have been utterly thrown down. *Shin jin datsu raku.*"

Nyojo replied the opposite: "*Datsu raku shin jin!*"[56]

At this moment the Master certified that the direction, the process, of Dogen's zazen was the correct one.

The significance of Nyojo's "*Datsu raku shin jin*" was to tell Dogen that he must continue his practice, going ever deeper, without ever stopping, for the rest of his life.

This too is nothing but a stage. The stage of Satori is not simply at one time, at one moment. Those of you who have received from me personally the kyosaku: if, at this time, you have received a big shock in your minds, then you have changed, you have woken up. This is Satori.

In Soto Zen, Satori means to return to the normal condition. My Master Kodo Sawaki always used to say this: Satori is the change which occurs in one's thoughts. All people are dogmatic, all people have their own personal thoughts, and so at the moment a person returns to the

Mondo continues on page 140.

---

[55] *Shin jin datsu raku*: Shin is mind; jin is body; datsu raku is to throw away, to throw down. Thus, literally: mind and body throw down!
[56] *Datsu raku shin jin*: Throw down body and mind!

OPPOSITE: *Zan mai*—Samadhi

三峡

normal condition, he finds everything in shock, everything turned about. This is Satori.

If you follow Dogen's Zen, then you must follow Dogen's Zen. If you follow Rinzai Zen, then you must follow Rinzai Zen. But what he did was to create a Soto-Rinzai Zen. I too could create the same thing. But I follow exactly the Zen of Dogen. Exactly, exactly.

Dogen never said that you must get Satori. Concerning that episode I have talked about when Dogen heard Nyojo say "*Shin jin datsu raku*" to the sleeping monk, the Rinzai sect claim that at this moment Dogen got Satori. But Dogen never said so. He never said: "At this time I got Satori." Nor did he ever write it. Mad people cannot understand that they are mad, for madness cannot be observed or experienced consciously. And, likewise, Satori cannot be observed or experienced consciously either. Nor can it be certified subjectively. Anyway, Dogen always said that you must not wait for Satori. He always said that zazen was Satori.

But Master Yasutani always makes this mistake. "You must get Satori," he would say.

For the American people Zen has become very complicated. There is Soto Zen, Rinzai Zen, Alan Watts Zen, Yasutani Zen, and they are all spreading.

If I wanted I could make all my disciples great Roshis right this minute. I could give you my certification, and right this minute you would become great Masters. Because I am related very exactly to the Transmission. The General Superintendent of Soto knows that my Zen is authentic and exact. They have certified it. So also has Kodo Sawaki certified it.

Philippe, you must read Doshu Okubo. Have you read him?

REPLY: Yes, I read him.

Session Four: August 23 – August 31, 1977

> MASTER: So you understand. You are happy.
> With true Masters there are no mistakes. With Rinzai Master Eido, who has a Rinzai Dojo in New York, there are no mistakes.[57]

One point in the cosmic system
Don't move, don't move. Body moves, mind moves.

If mind moves, receive the kyosaku and you will be able to stop the moving of the mind. You can experience this. When mind moves, body moves unconsciously. Minds which want to move, minds which want to stand up, are the minds of those here who wait for the end of zazen.

The study of dance—at the Santa Lucia—is very interesting. Mind moves, body follows . Body follows mind completely. Dancing is not moving of the body; it is moving of the mind. It starts from mind, not body. Dance is the expression of the mind. So when one dances, one cannot observe the body. One cannot understand one's veritable face.

During zazen we can observe our mind. We can control our face. We can control our body. During sleep body movement stops. The body, in sleep, has no tension, and so it does not move. During zazen, though, the body is in complete attention, it is living, and yet it does not move. Because body controls mind.

Christ's Communion with God was almost the same as Buddha's Satori under the Bodhi Tree. Almost the same. The fundamental cosmic power entered into Christ's body—as the Holy Spirit. In the case of Buddha, because of his earlier life of asceticism, he experienced nothingness of body. But continuing zazen under the Bodhi Tree—for nine days—his body woke up. It was not nothing. On the ninth day, at dawn,

---

[57] Today, Master Eido is strongly criticized and was even excommunicated by his own master for having several sexual relationships with his female disciples.

Buddha looked up at the morning star shining brightly, and his body woke up. "I am one point in the cosmic system." All existences, all Dharmas, exist, but they are the realization of all the cosmos together. Buddha woke up to the fundamental cosmic power. He became himself—he became the realization of the cosmos.

Do not move, neither with the body nor the mind
Don't move, don't move. People moving, minds moving. I ask those who move: what is moving? The mind? Or the body? This is a koan. Your pain will disappear with this koan.

Chukai![58]

As soon as I move, others move. Just like rats in a dark room.

∼

[With kinhin now over, the Master continues his kusen.]

I have conserved and protected a poem hand-lettered by Kodo Sawaki. It is a poem by the great Master Jiun. Jiun was a Shingon monk. Still, he practiced zazen every day. He was always doing zazen.

> *If mind moves, the mountain, the river, and the great earth move. If mind moves not, the birds, the animals, the blowing wind, and the drifting clouds move not. When in Mushin, we are in the highest happiness, we are in eternal life. When we think too much, when there is no concentration of mind, sickness arises, suffering appears. If we are in peace with the earth and the sky and the entire cosmos, we live one thousand autumns, ten thousand springs.*

---

[58] *Chukai*: To cease administering the kyosaku, to stop the kyosaku. When the Master says "Chukai," the Kyosaku-men replace the kyosakus on the altar below the statue of the Buddha. Once this is done, the small bell is struck twice and everyone stands up for kinhin.

Session Four: August 23 – August 31, 1977

My Master Kodo Sawaki liked this poem very much, and he kept it until he died. I too like it. Until today this poem has been a big koan for me.

~

In contemporary civilization people are always moving. But right now, here in this Dojo, there are more than two hundred people sitting without movement. Such a thing is utterly unknown in modern times. Two hundred people a week, for four weeks, sitting in zazen without moving. The children, who sometimes do zazen with us, become quiet. The dog too becomes quiet. And this, at the end of the twentieth century—it is a great mystery.

If body moves not, mind moves not. Look not at those whom you like, nor at those whom you dislike, and your mind does not move. Hear not the sound of a car, the sound of thunder, and your mind will not move. Touch not, and your mind moves not. This is in the *Hannya Shingyo*.

Of course, in daily life, when it is necessary to act, we must act. So if, after this sesshin, you continue to practice zazen, you can develop the habit of controlling your actions, and so you can control the mind. And thus you can become free and tranquil, even while in movement.

~

Kinhin!
Stretch the knees.
Massage! [59]

[With the massages over, everyone returns to his or her place.]

~

---

[59] During the sesshins, often the Master conducts special massages.

Concentrate. If you do not concentrate, then you will have to continue zazen for thirty more minutes. But if you concentrate, and in so doing maintain a good posture, then I will make the zazen shorter.

After a massage your bodies have changed—you can feel the change—and so it is easier now to do zazen. Your brains are no longer complicated; there is no thinking; the body is light. Some here are in a state of ecstasy. Ecstasy is not Satori.

Theology without practice is empty
During zazen we can become the Holy Spirit. But once zazen is over, all go about putting their Holy Spirit on display—by their manners, their ceremonious attitudes, their language. This is bonno-mind. Once zazen is over, everybody quickly returns to bonno-mind.

Of course, intellectual understanding is necessary. But then it must be realized through our actions. Intellectual understanding stems from the frontal brain: "Yes, I understand. I know." To practice this understanding, however, is another matter. We forget to do so.

Theology, ethical teachings, the sutras, have always been complicated and abstract; and this being so, they are difficult to put into practice. For the Christian religions today, a practical theology is necessary. So I hope that, through living religious experience, a new theological practice will come into being. Not an old practice—a new one.

Shikantaza, the complete concentration while in zazen, has been practiced and penetrated by all the Masters of the Transmission. And transmission of this religious experience is, in Zen, of utmost importance. Nevertheless, each experience undergone by each Master is different.

Zazen and *samu*[60] together are very important. I like samu myself, and would like to do it with you. But during a sesshin it is

---

[60] *Samu*: Concentration on manual work such as scrubbing floors, cleaning out pots and pans, sweeping the walks, etc.

Session Four: August 23 – August 31, 1977

difficult. What must I do, clean out the toilet? Sometimes I do this—this is a good samu for me.

I am impressed with Christ's life. In his thirty or so years of life, he gave very few conferences. And the education he gave his disciples lasted for only three years. Christ lived most of his life as a carpenter. It is the same with me: I was a businessman until I was fifty. I am most impressed with Christ. I have forgotten most of the Bible now, but I remember the Last Supper. Christ washed the feet of his disciples. "Please, as I do for you," he said to them, "as by my example—you will do likewise in the future."

But religious people today forget this.

I want to wash S's feet. But they are too big. E's[61] also, they are very big. I want to give my disciples massages. When I first came to Paris, I gave massages from morning until night.[62] But it was difficult. Women's buttocks and legs are very large usually.

∼

[The two bells announcing kinhin are struck, and everyone begins kinhin. After the one bell ending kinhin is struck, the Master says:] Everybody here is trying to shorten the zazens. They walk slowly back to their places; they look at the others as they walk. And then they wait for everyone to sit down so that they can be the last to sit. Theology without practice is empty.

∼

---

[61] E and S are two of the Master's close disciples.

[62] To come into contact with the people of Paris (and also in order to make a living), the Master gave massages when he first arrived in France. In this he was like Eka, the Second Patriarch, who upon receiving the Transmission from Bodhidharma became first a butcher, then a street sweeper.

Theology without prayer—without nonmotivated prayer—is empty.

In October, when I visit the Christian monasteries in Italy, I will explain to the monks there that the highest motivation is zazen. Mushotoku. To ask something of God is not necessary. Communication with God must be done unconsciously, automatically and naturally.

To practice zazen is better than to listen to conferences given by theologians. The great theologian of the Middle Ages, Thomas Aquinas, understood the limits of theology. "Through theology we cannot understand God," he once said. "Through theology we can only understand what God is not." Thomas Aquinas understood. Through his own personal religious experience, he understood that God is beyond human intelligence. It is the same with Zen. Abstract concepts cannot transmit living experience. Abstract concepts cannot educate.

That which is most important is to practice—by ourselves. Theology, in the future, will be like this. For even if we understand theology, theology without practice is ineffective.

Zazen is the highest attitude of prayer.

～

Kaijo!
To indicate the hour we strike the kaijo. Ten strikes indicate ten o'clock. After the kaijo, we strike the metal in the kitchen, along with the wooden fish at the entrance to the Dojo. Then one stroke of the bell to indicate the end of zazen.

Stronger, kyosaku!
Some people here have a poor posture. Especially the new people from Germany. Correct posture is very important. I do not permit people to do zazen squatting on their knees in the Japanese style, nor in the Yoga position with hands on knees. You must sit in the lotus or the half-lotus.

Session Four: August 23 – August 31, 1977

New people from Germany: I want to welcome you.[63] And those who understand none of the languages—please try your best anyhow.

This morning when I arrived in the Dojo without the bell,[64] many people were not seated in their places. This is not exact Zen. There is no need to wait for me.

Only today and tomorrow morning are left of this sesshin. A week-long sesshin is what is really needed. But because of all the new people who keep coming, I have arranged it so that the first part of the week is set aside for preparation. I am using the soft Zen education. True traditional Zen is much more severe.

Those who don't follow the rules of this Dojo must do zazen outside. [Apparently some individuals, despite the Master's words, are still sitting in an improper posture.] Those who sit in the Yoga position, those who cannot sit in the lotus or half-lotus, those who cannot sit in the proper posture, they must sit outside the Dojo. And when the Master passes behind you in the morning (*Kentan*[65] it is called), it is necessary that you do gassho. When I pass behind you, I too am doing gassho—though in Japanese Temples it is not necessary for the Master to do gassho in return. But I do it because I do it for you. Some people do not do gassho. But they must understand. They must do it.

They understand. But they just don't want to do it. This is the worst. These people must receive the kyosaku—and then out. In Zen one must abandon ego. One must leave off attachment. One must go with the cosmic order.

---

[63] All talks, all kusens, are given in English and translated simultaneously into French. However, on this occasion the Master had a simultaneous translation done into German as well.

[64] During zazen, the Master's arrival is announced by the striking of the little hand bell, the inkin. On this day, however, the Master arrived for zazen unannounced.

[65] *Kentan*: During Kentan the Master observes those who are present—he examines their postures and their dress, he looks to see if anyone is sick, etc. See Glossary.

ZEN & KARMA

Don't move! The German boy here is always moving. Maybe he does not understand English. Or French. If he were clever, he would understand by now, because every time he has moved during the past zazens, I have said "Pas bouger, pas bouger." Even me, I understand this much.

If the atmosphere of the Dojo is not good, is not exact, then many will make mistakes; many will make errors. This is why many here right now are sitting with insufficient tension.

The Godo (the educator), the Kyosaku-man, or the Master must give the rensaku to everyone. Everyone here must receive it. But with more than two hundred people present now, it will be difficult to give it to all of them.

∼

Kyosaku!

Stephane, Alain—you must help the other two Kyosaku-men give the kyosaku. Each person must receive it.

[The kyosaku is now being administered.]

Stronger! There is no need to be soft. There is no need to be diplomatic. When giving the kyosaku, you must be mushin.

[The Master has risen, and taking up a kyosaku, he joins the other Kyosaku-men. He gives the kyosaku.]

During these last moments you must have patience. The last moments are very important. When you go through difficulties, you progress.

∼

Chukai!

Kinhin!

There is too much coughing, too much nose-blowing in the Dojo whenever kinhin starts. There is no need to go "Achhchoo!" and to make other strange noises. Minds are not quiet.

The great Master Isan tested his disciples by the sounds of their voices. By the sounds they made when clearing their throats.

By the sounds of their cough. In Zen, one must take care of even the sound of one's cough. Some people here do not sound so good. [The Master makes a cat-like cough:] Iiitshi! Iiitshi! Anyway, Master Isan gave the Shiho by the sounds of their voices.

[The bell announcing the end of kinhin has sounded, and everyone returns to his place.]

∼

For those who have a coughing problem, when they wake up before the morning zazen they must drink hot water. Or take something sweet, like sugar or syrup. And those who still can't stop coughing must tape their mouths closed.

Nor is it necessary to have coughing competitions in the Dojo. Dogen forbade even zazen competition, so coughing competitions are certainly not necessary. I know how it goes: one does it, the person next to him does it too, and so it goes on, right down the line. Here is the mistake of democracy.

God is in our minds, not in the sky
Christ said: "God exists in our mind."

Someone asked him: "When will the Kingdom of God come?"

"The Kingdom of God does not come in a visible form," he replied.

This is impossible to explain. Look here, this is the Kingdom of God. God's Kingdom exists in the mind. The sky exists in proximity, not far away, not in heaven. It is the same with paradise. Christ understood Zen. It is the same. God does not exist in the sky. God is everywhere. So why, after Christ's death, have so many mistaken notions come about? God is everywhere. Here and now know where Christ is. Here and now—this is important for you.

In the Occident, God dwells in heaven. So it is said in Christian prayers: "God is in heaven." Westerners see God in terms which are too poetic, too objective. Western philosophers, psychologists, scientists, theologians and artists look too much to the outside; they look objectively, and so they forget to look to the inside, to look subjectively. Westerners do not look deeply enough into their own minds. Zazen is different. Zazen is not for outside show. Zazen is not a decoration. Zazen is to look profoundly, intimately inside oneself. Zazen is to discover God within your inner mind. It has nothing to do with heaven.

Schiller, the German writer, and Beethoven too—even they perpetuated this mistaken notion. Beethoven, inspired by one of Schiller's poems, incorporated it into his *Ninth Symphony:*

Let yourself be embraced
By this kiss of all the world.
Brothers, beyond the arch of stars
He is surely living, dear Father.

You millions—are you broken?
Isn't it yet evident that there is a creation in this world?
You must seek Him beyond the arch of stars,
For over the stars He is enthroned.

I like the *Ninth Symphony*. And this poem, it is beautiful. People love beautiful poems, images, imagination; but what these poems say is mistaken. Poetry, the theater—they all make mistakes. Why must we look into the stars; why must we search for God up in the stars? Why in the stars? Well, it doesn't matter, because people don't really look anywhere correctly, anyhow. But why does Schiller say this? I can see very well that God exists in my mind. Beyond the arch of stars—Yes, God is there. Maybe.

A pretty poem. Nonetheless, poems such as this become popular, and so eventually people come to believe them—that God is in heaven.

This poem is not great and joyful. It is sad. It is made for crying. It creates a longing for eternity, and so Europeans will never—never for eternity—find the real God. This is a sad European karma.

OPPOSITE: *Ki*—Cosmic energy, spirit

龍

Christ understood the true, the real God. He understood true Zen. No one else has understood the true God as did Christ. God exists in the mind. In your mind. "The Kingdom of God," wrote Luke, "exists in your mind."

Zen and Christianity, the East and the West, are like two separate highways. But sometimes I come across points of interchange, intersections, crossroads between the two. Deep ones.

If you do zazen, you will find the complete, the total Satori. The same Satori as Christ's. The same as Buddha's. The form is not the same, but in the end they are the same.

In Zen it is the return to the source which is developed. Zen means to return to the source, to the root, while in modern sciences there are only branches and flowers. And glory. Christianity has become glorious, like twinkling stars in the sky. But God—he is dead.

Here now, though, you are searching and finding God. Here you become accurate in your zazen, accurate in your posture. This in itself is the Kingdom of God. [Silence.]

Don't move, don't move. Swiss boy! Patience is important. You won't die. If you concentrate on your pain, the pain gets worse. Forget the pain. Put your mind elsewhere. Change your mind.

The object of concentration is very important. Not the Santa Lucia—not during the sesshin. Here-and-now zazen posture. Here is the true Kingdom of God. The true Santa Lucia. You don't know the meaning of Santa Lucia?

Training oneself in patience

During a sesshin, patience is very important. In the sutras, patience is regarded as the highest virtue, the highest concept. Patience is the most important commandment; it is much more efficient than any ascetic training. The merits of patience are infinite. During a sesshin—patience. Sesshin sometimes means training in patience.

It is very difficult to always have patience—particularly during a sesshin. The pain (everybody ends up in pain), the kyosaku (egoistic people find the kyosaku very painful), the food (which is not so good—no meat, no wine, no whiskey), sex (which is hard to have), and the silence (which, during mealtimes, is absolute) make it difficult to always have patience.

But with patience—with its practice—ego disappears. And at this instant the Santa Lucia penetrates the body. Santa Lucia means saintly light. It is not necessary to go to the Santa Lucia. Zazen is Mushotoku.

∼

Kinhin!

When putting your foot down, stretch the knee. Stretch the muscles around the waist.

Those whom I touch—these people are doing a good kinhin. [The Master passes between the rows of people walking in kinhin, picking out those with good postures.]

Stop. Look at those whom I have indicated. Look at their postures. The postures of their hands. The position of their chins. The way they step. Most important is their dignity. Very beautiful. Certainly better than Christ's kinhin.

[With kinhin over, several people go off to the toilet.]

People must not go to the toilet during zazen. Go before. Of course, I permit them to anyway. Otherwise they would only go on their zafus.

To have patience when one wants to go *pipi* is very difficult—especially during zazen. It is even more difficult to hold back from going to the toilet than to hold back from coughing.

I know because I had the experience during a sesshin at Eiheiji. I had a weakness of the bladder, and the more I tried to be patient, the worse it got. As it is forbidden to stand up during zazen, and as there was no way of escaping unnoticed (everyone knew me—I had the best posture in Eiheiji), I tried hard to be patient. I pressed my pipes closed by pushing down on them with my buttocks. Mind, at such a time, is in a state of coma. I visited paradise—and so had to be helped out by the

Kyosaku-man. I had fallen into a coma because of my patience. (This has become a well-known story in Japan. Like the time when I attacked the Kyosaku-man in Kamakura—that too is well known.)

During conferences too it is not so easy to hold oneself back when one wants to go to the toilet—particularly when it is very cold. Like the time when I was holding a big conference in Geneva—it was during the middle of winter, and the room was very cold, and as Ingred, the pianist, had given me a lot of beer beforehand, I was always excusing myself to go *pipi*. About every five minutes. And even later that evening, while Ingred was driving me around on a tour of Munich, I had to go again. So my secretary told the driver: "Stop the car; Sensei wants to go *pipi*." The driver replied that it was not possible to stop now, as we were in the middle of traffic. I tried to be patient, but it wasn't possible. "If you don't stop, I will go in the car," I warned. "*Attendez! Attendez!*"[66] the driver kept saying. Anyway, when the car got stuck in a traffic jam, I jumped out. I escaped. In front of me stood the famous Munich Opera House. Lots of ladies and gentlemen standing about the entrance to the Opera stared in amazement at me as I pushed my way through them. I must have looked funny to them—with my strange clothes, my shaved head, and the panicked expression on my face. Anyway, I found the restroom in the Opera.

Everyone has experienced this problem. But during zazen it is the worst. I've practiced patience for forty years, and so I'm not afraid of anything—not even of a rain of bullets in wartime. But when it comes to having patience when I must go *pipi*, for this I am afraid.

∼

---

[66] *Attendez*: Wait!

Kinhin!

The posture of kinhin is the basic posture found at the root of all the martial arts. Of all of them. Kinhin is not the same as walking. Tension, no tension. Look on one point, see everything. If you acquire the habit of kinhin, your regular walking will have dignity.

∼

Kyosaku!

Too much tension in zazen is not good. Nor is ecstasy, nor is sleepiness.

[Thirty minutes have passed in silence. Then:]

Chukai!

Mondo!

MONDO

QUESTION: Why do some people, even in childhood, have bad karma?

MASTER: Because of your ancestors; because of you, yourself, before. In Buddhism, one's ancestors are not considered to have much influence. In a sutra it is written that it is a matter of one's own proper karma—before this world. Karma does not come out of nothing. It is the same as the law of Mendel. While in the uterus, from embryo (from amoeba) to infant, we cover a span of one hundred million years. While in the uterus, we experience the entire history of man. So each person's experiences are different. And so different karmas arise. Understand?

QUESTION: What is the difference between following the ego and following the cosmic order?

ZEN & KARMA

MASTER: You don't know? To follow the ego is to be egoistic. To follow the ego is to follow your desires.

I am not much of a moralist. I don't deny desires. I too sometimes have them. Desires are sometimes necessary, and some desires are not so bad. In any case, you must sublimate your desires, for it is important that they be given a higher dimension.

But to attach oneself to one's desires, no. When, in your mind, you cannot realize something, when you cannot succeed as you would like, and your mind suffers, becomes angry, afraid—this is no good. But when you follow the cosmic order, even with all the world against you, your mind remains tranquil, free. When my last secretary left, my inside-mind remained free. And so it would be even if my present secretary, Anne-Marie, left. If all of you, if all my disciples leave, and if I no longer have enough to eat, my inside-mind will still be free.

You people, you are always saying: "Since Sensei is not attached, since he always follows the cosmic order, why does he get angry? Why does he desire things?" It is natural. It is outside-mind. But inside-mind is not so. Inside-mind is not very angry. You say: "Sensei was angry a moment ago, and now he is smiling." Mind is always changing because there is no attachment. Mind is always free. Mushotoku.

The outside-mind is not the same. Your education and so on. And then, of course, you must live. So sometimes you must be diplomatic. With desires too—even when there aren't any. Be like this, even when you drink whiskey. This is wisdom.

QUESTION: D.T. Suzuki, whose works on Zen are so widely read in the United States and elsewhere—what do you think of his understanding of Zen?

Session Four: August 23 – August 31, 1977

MASTER: D.T. Suzuki has the merit, the distinction, of having introduced Zen to the large American public. But on the other hand, Suzuki did not experience zazen—except maybe a little bit in his youth—so he cannot answer such a question. Suzuki's works are psychological and philosophical. Not true Zen. Suzuki was very deeply into Oriental and Japanese philosophy, particularly Mahayana Buddhism and Rinzai. But on the final deep point he had no experience, so one cannot really understand Zen through D.T. Suzuki.

D.T. Suzuki did not do zazen at all. I have never heard of anyone who was educated in zazen by Professor Suzuki. Not even in Japan. Has anyone ever seen Professor Suzuki do zazen? No, no, no. No one. He was a professor, not a monk. Suzuki did not study the Shobonenzo deeply. He only used it. He did not understand true Zen. He did not experience zazen. It is like looking at an apple painted on paper—you can't eat it. Understand?

QUESTION: In your opinion, what are you? A Master? A religious leader? A philosopher?
MASTER: Ha ha! Good question. I sometimes wonder myself. But what you are doing is limiting by categories. You cannot do this. It is the same thing with the four stages, the four steps [to Satori] I spoke of earlier.

Sometimes I am a philosopher. Sometimes a religious person. Sometimes a monk. Sometimes an educator. Sometimes a whiskey-drinker.

A great historian can understand. It is the disciples who decide. Most important are the disciples. If great disciples arise (like those around Christ), then you have great Masters. (As with Christ—it was the disciples who made Christ great.) However, this is not so with present-day professors, present-day doctors—these people are weak.

ZEN & KARMA

> Even if I am not great, if my disciples become great, then so do I. This is true: disciples decide. Today they say that Deshimaru has become a true great Master. So now it is the same with my own Master, Kodo Sawaki. No one knew Kodo Sawaki during his time, not even in Japan. But today he is famous.
>
> I am a religious man. I concentrate completely on Shikantaza. Until death. This is my only object.
>
> I want to stay at my Temple in Avalon[67] and at the Dojo in Paris until I am eighty or ninety, doing sesshins with the people who visit me there. And in the end I want to rest in the ground of Avalon. This is my idea.
>
> When I die, then here-and-now: only this. True Zen monk. Understand?
>
> How much time is left? Good. We'll do a little more zazen.

"I believe more in the Bible than in the sutras…"

In the Bible there are some excellent koans. When I was young I was very impressed with the Bible, with the flowery poetry of the Evangels, with Christ, with his life and by his words. "God's Kingdom exists in your mind," said Christ. In Japanese this phrase sounds very pretty. And also: "Paradise is within hand's reach." On the other hand, I did not much like Buddhist vocabulary. My mother was always talking Buddhism, and in the *Amida Buddha Sutra*, which she often quoted to me, it is written that the Pure Land exists somewhere far off in the West—at a distance of three thousand million *do*. I did not much care for this saying; it was too hard to believe.

---

[67] The Temple in Avalon is located about one hundred miles south of Paris. It is actually a monastery, and it was built by the Master's disciples.

Session Four: August 23 – August 31, 1977

Today in my room, the American boy, Philippe Coupey, was telling me how much he disliked the sound of Biblical words, and that the mere sound of them disturbed him.

Young people all want to escape from their traditional religions. Like myself. When I was young I did not like the old traditional sutras. I liked the Bible instead. "God's country exists in one's mind." These few words woke me up. They gave me Satori. In those days I believed much more in the Bible, with its fancy leather binding, than I did in my mother's old worn-out sutra book. I liked knives and forks, too—much more than chopsticks. And so with the Evangelists.

But the Evangels, which are merely poetic and beautiful and not at all practical, did not satisfy me for very long.

A Protestant minister—a Japanese man—gave me many Christian books to read. And some of them were considered very rare. Others were secret texts, and some were forbidden reading for Christians. One of the texts he gave me—a text which had been uncovered in 1819 by a Christian missionary somewhere in Constantinople and was written in Greek—dealt with the teachings of the twelve Apostles. This particular text dealt specifically with the rules of practical life for Christian Adepts. Anyhow, Catholics and Protestants alike had this text suppressed. Others too—practical texts on Christianity, on Christ's true life, on practice in daily living—have likewise been suppressed and still remain so, even today. This is a sorry story in the history of European civilization. I think so.

If I use koans, I do not find them in the traditional Rinzai texts on koans. I find them, if I want, in the words of Christ.

"God's country," said Christ, "exists in your mind." So show it, please. Show it here and now. If the disciple fails to show it, I give him the kyosaku and tell him that he must continue zazen. To the next disciple I say: "Show it. Show that God's country exists within reach." This disciple shows his hand. I answer nothing—ku. Your hand is ku, empty. Why? If the disciple cannot answer, I give him the kyosaku. He too must continue zazen.

ZEN & KARMA

Christian Masters would, I think, do the same. This approach is more practical than theology. More practical than reading the Evangels. In my opinion, this is the true teaching of Christ.

Dogen's big koan, during his youth, had to do with his doubt concerning the teaching of Buddhism.

Dogen was educated in Tendai and in Rinzai—notably under the famous Master Eisai. And then he went on to China, visited many Rinzai temples, and met with many Rinzai Masters. But it was with the Soto Master Nyojo that Dogen finally received the Shiho. He returned to Japan with the intention of spreading the practice of zazen in his own country. And so he wrote the *Fukanzazengi*. (*Gi*, here, does not mean poem or sutra, but rather it means practical rules. So the *Fukanzazengi* is quite different from the Bible, or from the Evangelists.)

A strong practice is necessary
"The way exists everywhere," Dogen wrote on the first page of the *Fukanzazengi*. (It is the same as with God, who exists everywhere.) . . . Since everybody has Buddha-nature anyhow, there is no need to practice. I thought this way myself at first.

English is a very convenient language. The word potential is very convenient. Today in my room, Alain Cassan, Philippe Coupey, Anne-Marie and I had a discussion, and in the discussion they taught me the meaning of the English word "potential." Potential. Potential power. Philippe said that it comes from "potent"—power. Without potent you are impotent. Once your potential is finished, even were you to play with yourself, you would still remain impotent. So, though you may have the potential nature of Buddha, the potential Holy Spirit, it becomes impotent without practice.

Yesterday a woman told me that she had the Holy Spirit. Certainly, but without practice this Holy Spirit cannot be realized. Fundamental cosmic power—it exists everywhere potentially. Fundamental cosmic potential. It fills the cosmos. But without practice, the fundamental cosmic potential becomes mere imagination, an idea, a decoration, a poem, a marionette.

Session Four: August 23 – August 31, 1977

To do zazen is to return to the normal condition. The zazen posture is potential. In *Ku soku ze shiki* of the *Hannya Shingyo*, the ku is potential. But once realized, the ku becomes phenomenon. While dancing at the Santa Lucia, there is no impotence. Everything dances, even the hair. So you have *Ku soku ze shiki*. On returning to the Dojo, you sit in zazen and maybe you become quiet. Then you have *Shiki soku ze ku*.

Potentiality is necessary. Thus bonno becomes Bodhi, becomes wisdom. And, contrarily, depending upon circumstances, upon interdependence, Bodhi (or Satori) can become bonno.

Bad karma, bad circumstances necessitate a strong and an accurate practice. Dogen, who had had a deep, profound experience and was himself a great, great religious Master, said that it is necessary that one's practice be strong. All great religious Masters have had a hard practice, and with this hard practice, their interdependences, their karma have changed into good interdependences, good karma.

If your legs are in pain, ask for the kyosaku. This way, with two areas in pain instead of just one, the pain is cut in half, and so it decreases.

Ideas of time

During zazen, time passes, passes. And then there is the bell. It is not necessary to wait for the bell. Time passes with exactitude.

Dogen, in his *Shobogenzo*, devoted a chapter to this question of time. *Uji*. Uji signifies both existence and time, and being-time.

Jaspers, whom I have met personally, read Dogen's chapter on Uji and was deeply impressed and surprised by it. I have been told that he said, "If I were to start my life over again, I would not write books—I would sit in silence." Heidegger too read this chapter on Uji and was likewise impressed with it.

As this chapter of Dogen's is very profound and difficult, I will explain it simply and briefly.

There are three notions of time. One of them is the general common everyday sense of time—that is, past time, present time, and future time. Another notion of time is subjective time, or stream of time. For instance, put your foot on the bottom of a riverbed, and though your foot remains fixed in the same spot in the river, you will see the water of the river flowing by, flowing by. The reverse is so too—that is, the flow can come from the future, through the present, into the past. For instance, when you sit in a moving train, the landscape passes you by in this fashion.

These first two notions of time are familiar to Western philosophy. Dogen, however, states that these two notions of time do not in fact exist, because past time is in the past and so does not exist. And likewise with future time, which is in the future and so does not exist either.

The third notion of time—and here we have the essence of Dogen's philosophy—shows time as nonexistent. All that is is the present. The present alone exists. The present moment, the now, the point, alone exists.

However, if you follow this point, if you concentrate on this now, on this now-now-now, then you have a straight, geometric-like line. You have the connections of eternity. You have eternity. Here now I am sitting in zazen. Here now I am sitting in the center of the cosmos. This is the center. Put a dot on a round ball, and however you look at it, this dot is everywhere the center. So here now is the center of the cosmos. Therefore, were only one person sitting here, his zazen would still spread throughout the cosmos. And, contrarily, the entire cosmos would concentrate itself in this one person. Do zazen alone, in solitude, and all existences are present, all existences are included. All things exist within ourselves, and each instant includes the entire world. And so each being is in direct relationship with the next, and each being is in interdependence with all humanity. This shows the relationship existing between time and space and the human being—and so we have the philosophy of Dogen. Therefore, we must give our entire body and soul, our entire body and mind, to the present moment. All action and all consciousness must be situated in the present moment. And so we must concentrate. Here and now.

This is not only realism—this is eternity. This is the infinite cosmos. This is not solitude; within this compassion is included the whole of humanity. Zazen is only one point. It is here and now, so it includes, potentially, all human beings, all existences, all the cosmos.

The posture of zazen is the true living Buddha

Everybody's posture this morning is very good. Please remember this posture when you are gone. It is the posture of the living God.

What is God? How was the posture of Christ? His face? His attitude? We can imagine it, but we cannot look at it. Certainly there are many fine drawings and paintings and sculptures of Christ and of Buddha, but these are only reproductions. I am always looking at your postures, during zazen and during kinhin. You are living. And so when I see your faces during kinhin, or your postures during zazen, I can find the true living Buddha, the living Christ.

But you must not be attached to Buddha. If the devil appears, hit the devil. If Buddha appears, hit Buddha. With the kyosaku. You must not be attached to anything. It is written in the *Shodoka* that all sages, God or Buddha, everything, must be wiped away—like lightning in the sky. You must not be attached. So at this moment what is Buddha? What is God?

Sometimes I say to you that your zazen posture, your kinhin posture, is better than Buddha's, better than Christ's. This is my imagination. Most everybody makes categories. What about Kant's imagination concerning God? Or Einstein's? Or Heidegger's? Or Beethoven's? Or Christ's? Which one is the truth? Everybody has something different to say about God. They are all categories.

There are many, many books written on Buddhism. And many commentaries have been written on Zen. By the Chinese and by the Japanese. And now by the Europeans and by the Americans. They are all writing on this subject now. These people have had little or no experience with zazen, they have not tasted the true essence of Zen, and yet they write, write,

write. It is like painting an apple on paper—you can't taste it. It is worse. The painter of the apple knows the taste of the apple because he has also eaten it. But these Zen commentators have not tasted the true essence of Zen, and yet they write about it.

When my Master, Kodo Sawaki, once asked me what it was which had most marked me, which had most impressed me in Zen, I replied that it was not the *Shobogenzo*, nor any of the books on the subject, nor even the Master's spoken words.

∽

"When I entered the Temple of Eiheiji," Kodo Sawaki once said, "I was about sixteen or seventeen years old. And at that time I could not become a monk, nor could I even wear the monks' clothes. I cleaned the Dojo, worked in the kitchen, and ran errands for vegetables, gobo[68] and the like. My room was located next to the kitchen, and it was narrow and dirty and stunk of vegetables, cucumbers, gobo, tamari and miso. And it was in this room where, when I had the time, I would practice zazen. I would sit in imitation of the monks who sat in the Dojo. One day the Tenzo caught me in zazen. The Tenzo was the Chief of the Kitchen, and he was third in line after the Temple Chief himself. He was a great figure in Eiheiji, but he was always angry with me, and so he was always hitting me. This time, though, he was so amazed that he stopped dead. Then he stepped backwards and did gassho. He had been struck by my posture. Talking very respectfully, the Tenzo said: "Here is the true sitting Buddha. Here is the true living Buddha."

"It was then," Kodo Sawaki said, "that I understood that the posture of zazen is the true living Buddha."

∽

---

[68] *Gobo*: Burdock.

OPPOSITE: *Mu ge ko*—Infinite illumination

豐年吉兆

Don't move . . . Have patience . . . There is only this morning left. Now and after breakfast.

You have the great good fortune to be doing zazen here like this. And now there is not much time left. Take this opportunity.

Satori is not important
[The kusen continues after kinhin.]

The zazen before kinhin was too long. Many people fell down. They were not patient. Long becomes short. And so now we have only a short time left. Good becomes bad; bad becomes good. "Receive one," wrote Dogen in the *Shobogenzo*, "lose one." When we lose one, at that moment we receive one. Everything is like this. In the *Hannya Shingyo we have fuzo fugen*—no increase, no decrease.

In Christianity, love is the most important factor. Yesterday during the mondo a woman kept insisting on love. Always talk about love, love, love. In Japanese it is *ai, ai, ai*. Of course, compassion in Buddhism is very important. But compassion is not love. In Buddhism love is completely a bonno. It is attachment. Yet for Christians love is very important. The love between God, Christ and myself. Love Christ. Love God.

My friend Father L, who lives in Japan, has informed me that he has changed from Rinzai to Soto. And now he has a Zen Dojo there, where he practices zazen. Still he understands nothing of Soto Zen. Christian Zen, yes. But not Soto Zen. Christianity is Christianity, Zen is Zen, and though of course we can find similarities between the two, one should go beyond them both. It is not necessary to become attached to Zen, to Buddha, God or Christ. Christian people, writes L, can never experience true Satori. I question this. L is always imagining Satori. In Soto, Satori is not so important. (I do not want to become God or Buddha, because then I could not drink whiskey, nor could I eat meat. Buddha died from poisoned intestines—from eating pork.) Anyway, Father L is always making categories. "How can a Christian have Satori?" he writes. People always want to make categories. Step one, step two, step three. Like a ladder. "God's love," writes L, "leads, leads, leads to Satori."

I am always saying that during zazen you must not run after Satori. Let all pass; attach yourselves to nothing. Not to love of God, nor even to his image. Otherwise you only limit God. A picture is only a picture. A sculpture is only a sculpture. Every day, when I look at your faces during kinhin, I can see the Buddha's face. When I look at your backs during zazen, I can find the true Buddha's posture.

A koan in solid bronze
The very last zazen—for those who have come for the last camp and for the permanents who have been here thirty-eight days. So please concentrate.

No, this is not the last zazen. This is only the last zazen here in Val d'Isere. There is no last zazen.

In the Corinthian text it is written as follows: "You are already dead—your life is hidden away in God, along with Christ." This is a koan, a Christian koan. "Your mind, during zazen, is as if within the coffin—your life becomes the cosmic potential." This is a Zen koan. This is my koan here in Val d'Isére.

At the entrance to the University of Komasawa sit two huge statues in zazen—my disciples who accompanied me to Japan have all seen them. To the right of the entrance is a statue of my Master, Kodo Sawaki. He is sitting in zazen in a *kolomo*[69] and Kesa. The posture of this statue, it has been said, is the posture of Buddha. To the left of the entrance is a statue of a nude young man—nude but for a Kesa-like material draped over his left shoulder. The young man in the sculpture has an almost wild look about him. "The Seated Dragon" is engraved below the statue.

To find a model for the statue of the wild-looking man, the sculptor presented himself to Kodo Sawaki. The sculptor was

---

[69] *Kolomo*: A monk's robe.

looking for the disciple with the strongest and the most correct posture.

Though I was only twenty-four years old at the time—and not even a monk yet—Kodo Sawaki asked me to pose. My Master overlooked others—monks of many years' standing—to choose me. So for three months I did zazen in the sculptor's studio. The studio was located in the outskirts of Tokyo, and Kodo Sawaki once came to visit us there. Examining the statue, he made some corrections. He corrected the position of the chin—he pushed it further in. He also corrected the hollow of the back. He hollowed it out some more, making it so that the buttocks protruded further to the rear.

During the exhibition, which was a big affair and crowded with influential people, many women placed gifts in front of the statue. Some left money, others burning incense. And then they did gassho.

After the exhibition we had the statue transported to my house. Due to lack of space, the statue was placed in the bedroom. My wife—we had just gotten married—was afraid of the statue, and she said: "This is not possible! How can we make love with such a statue sitting at the foot of our bed?"

I talked with Kodo Sawaki about it. "It is true," he said. "You must not do zazen in front of your wife. It will only scare her. It would be better if you left it off at the University."

Later, when I would visit Kodo Sawaki at the University where he gave conferences (at the time he was a professor at Kamasawa, as well as Godo at Sojiji), he would introduce me to the famous professors and to the other influential people often clustered about him as the model who had posed for the statue now sitting at the entrance to the University. "This statue," he would say, "is better than mine. It is even better than Buddha's." And to me he said, in reference to statues in general: "Real people are not like this. But once they are cast in bronze, they represent the highest people." This is a koan. I was impressed. Real people are never so perfect. I decided then that I had to become like this statue—and not only while in zazen.

Session Four: August 23 – August 31, 1977

Never have I forgotten this decision. It has become a koan for me—throughout my entire life. This sculpture was one of the original causes for my becoming a monk. An unconscious cause—I did not think about it. What I thought about was how I had to become like this statue. Whenever I was about to follow my bad karma, I would remember this statue; I would reflect on it. This statue guided me in my life—this statue which represented my body.

Today I forget my posture. I am not so attached anymore. Sometimes I correct my posture. Sometimes I concentrate on my kusens. During my kusens, when I stop to say: "Chin in, stretch the backbone, push the sky with the head, the ground with the knees," it is not only for you that I say this. It is also for me. I've continued the practice of zazen for more than forty years, so it is to my mind that I talk.

The posture of your body, the attitude of your mind—they are very important. So please remember this—remember yourselves as you are here now, during this last zazen in Val d'Isére. Posture and mind can be in unity. If posture is correct, mind is correct. If posture moves not, mind moves not. If posture is quiet, mind is quiet. Posture, attitude, behavior—they all influence the mind.

Finally, to finish, I wish you happiness and good health.

I am having you sit twenty minutes more. It is a present. An invisible present. From my heart.

To have patience during these last moments is very important . . . Today is a lovely day, so everyone moves . . . The Santa Lucia . . . The mountains . . . Home . . . Trip to Spain . . .

Kaijo!

APPENDIX

Changing Your Karma
by Philippe Rei Ryu Coupey

If you do zazen for an hour now, this action sows a seed which will generate a good and profound karma, the highest karma of all, from now to eternity.

—Taisen Deshimaru

Following his master Taisen Deshimaru, Philippe Rei Ryu Coupey has pursued the teachings of the Dharma and its transmission for more than thirty years, in particular clarifying the question of karma through the light of his own understanding. Here are a few short excerpts from this teaching.

One cannot escape one's karma
Karma, this is one's actions, with its causes and consequences. That applies to everyone, nobody can escape it. Even a great master cannot escape his karma. This is what Zen teaches.

During the course of one's existence, karma becomes complicated; there is work, full of competition, a relationship, children … For most people it is difficult to maintain a peaceful mind: we reject things, we desire, we regret, we become attached, and all of that has innumerable repercussions. In this way karma is the seed of another karma yet to come. Each action has its visible repercussions and hidden consequences.

Neither determinism nor fatalism
The law of karma does not imply determinism. Karma places the individual in a given situation, without offering a response to that situation.

This is not fatalism either. People are not prisoners of their karma. The teaching is very clear on this subject: you can change your karma. For this reason our teaching tells us that we are deeply free, even if we find ourselves behind bars. That means that we can cut our karma immediately and not follow the conditions that brought us to this point here and now.

We can transform our karma

Thanks to our practice, we lead our karma, change our karma, we change our lives, we change our behavior little by little, invisibly. We loosen the links of the law of karma.

Through our practice, we are not prisoners of our karma, we do not follow our karma, it is our karma that follows us. It is behind us and yet we are free to change what is in our past. If we only look in one direction our karma follows us in that direction.

Exceeding superficial representations

We always think that to simply cut our karma, we have to stop something. But it is not about stopping something, rather about creating something different, about transforming. In any case we are always in the process of creating karma.

In this work Deshimaru states that "from the karmic point of view, ancestors do not influence their descendants." That is to say that we are free of our parents, we are free of our ancestors … we are free of our karma. We are not slaves to our karma, we are its master. We only have to open our eyes to the retrospective effect of karma: when the son takes up the practice of realization, the father becomes the father of a Buddha.

By changing our karma, we change the karma of the world

We have very important work to do, not just for our personal karma, but for karma as a whole. Karma comes from millions of things—everything we have done in the past—that's why our civilization is in such a state. However, what interests us is not what has happened, but what *can* happen.

We should not allow ourselves to think that everything starts anew when we are born and the bad karma in our society has nothing to do with us. The essence of karma is not a personal thing, but we cannot say we are here for nothing: we are here for just that. When we are born, it is because what we have done is still there.

GLOSSARY

Bodhi – (tree) – Sanskrit. The tree under which the Buddha had the experience of awakening, at the end of forty-nine days of seated meditation.

Bodhidharma – (4th-5th century, Japanese. Daruma.) A disciple of the Indian master Hannyatara and the master of Eka. He is the first patriarch of Chinese Buddhism Ch'an and the twenty-eighth in the Indian lineage, uninterrupted since the Buddha himself.

Bodhisattva – Sanskrit. "An awakened being." Everyone can realise that they are this and can dedicate their life to helping others do the same, according to the vow the Bodhisattva makes whilst participating in real life. Nothing distinguishes the bodhisattva from others, yet his mind is "buddha."

Bonno – Japanese. *Bon* means something troubling, something that disturbs, and *no*, that which causes suffering, what torments. Generally, we translate *bonno* as "passions" although this term is a little restrictive. The *bonnos* are all the illusions, attachments and all other products of individual consciousness.

bonno soku bodai – The bonnos become satori.

Buddha – Sanskrit. "The awakened one." Used with a capital letter, this indicates the historical Buddha Shakyamuni, born in Kapilavastu in 536 BCE and who died in 483.

By extension, it is also: (1) The legendary Buddhas of the past, present and future. (2) An individual who has attained awakening. (3) Illumination or awakening. (4) "The principle of buddha," the fundamental cosmic power and/or the true nature of the universe, which is manifest in all its diverse forms.

Buddhism – "The religion of awakening" is one of the great spiritual and philosophical movements of humanity. It was founded in the 5th century BCE by the historical Buddha Shakyamuni. It is divided into two main branches. (*See* Mahayana and Hinayana.)

Chukai! – A word pronounced in the Dojo by the master to tell the person with the kyosaku to cease administering the kyosaku and replace it on the altar.

Daichi Sokei (1290–1366) – A Japanese master famous for his poetry. He received ordination as a monk from Kangan Gin, a disciple of Dogen, and later practised with Keizan for seven years. At the age of twenty-five, he went to China and stayed for eleven years. Coming back to Japan, he received transmission from Meiho Sotetsu, one of the heirs of Keizan.

Dharma – Sanskrit. The fundamental law, the universal order as it is manifest in the Way, but also the teaching, the Buddhist doctrine as given by the historical Buddha Shakyamuni.

Dogen (1200–1253) – A Japanese master, disciple of the Chinese master Nyojo and the master of Ejo. He developed Soto Zen in Japan and founded the temple of Eihei-ji. Son of a noble family, he studied Rinzai Zen and the *koan* method with Eisai and Myozen before going to China where he met his master, who certified him at the end of three years. Dogen is the author of the authoritative work, the *Shobogenzo*.

Dojo – Japanese. "*Do*" means the Way, "*jo*" the place. The place of practice.

Dokan – Japanese. The ring of the Way. The conscious repetition of actions in everyday life. Repetition of the posture, the attitude of body and mind as an uninterrupted practice. (see *gyoji*)

Glossary

Eiheiji – Japanese. "The monastery of eternal peace." One of the two principal monasteries of the Soto Zen school in Japan, the other being Sojiji. Founded in the 12th century by Master Dogen, it is situated to the north of the central part of Japan in the province of Fukui, notorious for the severity of its winters.

Eno – (*Hui Neng* 638–713. Chinese.) The 6th patriarch of Zen, disciple of master Konin (*Hung-jen*, Chinese.) Eno played a great role in the spread of *Ch'an* in China. According to tradition, Eno was illiterate and awakened when he heard a monk reciting this sentence from the Diamond Sutra: "When the mind rests on nothing, the true mind appears."

Fukanzazengi – Japanese. "Universal guidelines for the practice of zazen." The very first text of Master Dogen, written in 1227 a little after his return from China and considered the backbone of his teaching.

Fuse – Japanese. (*Dana* – Sanskrit.) Gift, alms. The action of spontaneously offering something material, one's energy or wisdom. One of the fundamental Buddhist virtues, one of the six "ways of perfection." (*paramita*)

Gassho – Japanese. "Palms of the hands joined." A gesture of reverence and respect, hands together about ten centimetres from the face, the ends of the fingers level with the nose, the forearms horizontal.

Genjo koan – Japanese. The title of the first chapter of the *Shobogenzo* of Dogen, composed in 1233. It deals essentially with the relationship between practice and the realization of the ultimate truth.

Godo – The master in the absence of the master. The monk or nun in charge of teaching.

Han – A piece of wood struck before and after a sitting of zazen.

Gyoji – Continual practice, without beginning or end. Regularity in practice.

Hannya Shingyo – Japanese. (Sanskrit, *Maha Prajna Paramita Hridaya.*) The Sutra of Great wisdom, also called the Heart Sutra. It is chanted in all Zen temples after *zazen*. This very brief sutra is the "heart" and the essence of the Mahayana teaching.

Hinduism – Hinduism is a religion composed of a number of beliefs, rituals and precepts – starting in the 3rd century BCE – sustained by the "universal cosmic law with no beginning." The obtaining of liberation (*moksha*) from the cycle of reincarnations (*samsara*) is the ultimate goal of all philosophies and all Indian mystical techniques.

Hinayana – The Small Vehicle. This term has a derogatory connotation, used by the followers of Mahayana Buddhism to describe the Buddhist trends which seek liberation for all individuals from *samsara*. It is equally known as "The Buddhism of the South" because of its geographic establishment in South-East Asian countries (Sri Lanka, Thailand, Burma, Cambodia and Laos). It is based by and large on an ideal of purity, the extinguishing of passions, attained by following a strict moral code. Its ideal is the figure of the *arhat*. Today it is represented by current Theravada, which describes itself as the original Buddhism.

Hishiryo –Japanese. Beyond thinking and non-thinking. This means thinking from the innermost depths of non-thinking. Beyond personal consciousness, following the cosmic order. With *shikantaza* and *mushotoko*, *hishiryo* makes one of the three pillars of the teachings of Kodo Sawaki and Taisen Deshimaru.

Glossary

Hoko Zan Mai – Japanese. "Samadhi of the precious mirror." This poem by Zen Master Tozan (died 869) is one of the four ancient essential Zen texts along with the *Shinjinmei*, the *Shodoka* and the *Sandokai*.

Hypothalamus – The central brain, instinctive, primitive, as opposed to the frontal brain, rational, and intellectual.

Ikebana – Japanese floral arrangement.

Innen – *In* is cause and *en* is karma, or interdependence. Every action is produced in harmony with both "in" and "en."

I shin den shin – Japanese. A fundamental idea of Zen, which describes the transmission beyond the scripture and intellectual understanding, from the mind of the master to that of the disciple. Kodo Sawaki once gave as an equivalent, "from heart-mind to heart-mind."

Kaijo! – Japanese. Literally "open the sounds." Announces the end of zazen and the beginning of the ceremony.

Kanji – Japanese. Chinese ideograms used in written Japanese.

Karma – Sanskrit. "Action." The law of universal causality. The totality of our acts and their consequences. Karma is created by the action of the body, the mouth and the mind. Karma is the law of cause and effect, and from this flows transmigration and *samsara* (the cycle of rebirth).

Kesa – Japanese. (Sanskrit, *keshaya*.) The monk's robe. The great robe made of many scraps of fabric, carefully assembled. Given by the master at the time of ordination, the *kesa* is an object of faith and veneration. It symbolises transmission and belonging to a lineage uninterrupted from the disciples of the Buddha, existence in a dimension which transcends the small self.

Ki – Japanese. (Chinese, *Chi*.) According to Taoist philosophy, vital energy, life force, the cosmic spirit which penetrates and animates all things. In the human body, it accumulates in the region of the navel (*kikai tanden* "the ocean of breath"). By extension, each individual master's way of teaching Zen.

Kiai! – A shout used in martial arts. An expression of ki. The process of verbalizing activity.

Kikai tanden – Japanese. The center of vital energy, also called the *hara*, situated just below the navel. In Zen, as in the martial arts, energy freed of tension and personal will concentrates and manifests itself in the *kikai tanden*.

Kinhin – Japanese. A slow walk to the rhythm of the breath, practised between two sittings of zazen.

Kito – Japanese. A ceremonial sutra for the recovery of the sick.

Koan – Japanese. Literally "public case." A sentence, word or gesture which leads to an understanding of the truth, used a lot in Rinzai Zen as a means of letting go of mental activity.

Kontin – Japanese. A state of drowsiness or lethargy during zazen.

Ku – Japanese. (*Sunyata*, Sanskrit.) Often translated as "empty" or "emptiness" as opposed to *"shiki"* or phenomena. However, *ku* and *shiki* are one. *Ku* indicates the infinite, the unborn from whence everything that is born and finite proceeds and returns. It is the place of transformation. It is the origin, the common identity without which differences (phenomena) could not exist. *Shiki sokuze ku, ku sokuze shiki*: phenomena become (are) emptiness, emptiness becomes (is) phenomena. Emptiness is form, form is emptiness.

Glossary

Kusen – Japanese. Oral teaching given in the dojo by the master during zazen. Teaching which is addressed directly to the deep consciousness of the practitioners, without being processed by the intellect. It seems that while *kusen* is used in the lineage of masters Kodo Sawaki and Deshimaru, other lineages prefer lectures *(teisho)*.

Kyoshi – Japanese. A grade of priest in the institution of Soto Zen. There are eight grades of *kyoshi*, and the four lowest are obtained after spending many months in a monastery. To obtain one of the four higher grades, one must be recommended. Also, their number is limited.

Kyosaku – Japanese. "The stick of awakening." A stick whose strikes are administered during zazen to the shoulders of the practitioner – or more exactly on the trapezius, the muscular area between the neck and the shoulder – generally when they ask for it. The *kyosaku* is a method of helping the practitioners to find their normal state, dissipating lethargy *(kontin)* or calming agitation *(sanran)*.

Mahayana – Sanskrit, "The Great Vehicle." One of the two branches of Buddhism, the other being Hinayana. Mahayana appeared in the 1st century BCE. Its purpose is to liberate all beings whilst postponing one's individual liberation. This attitude is incarnated in the Bodhisattva, who has taken the vows and whose principal virtues are compassion *(karuna)* and the development of the mind of awakening *(bodhicitta)*. Its roots are found mainly in Tibet, China, Korea and Japan.

Mondo – Japanese. Questions and answers between disciples and master, not in the intimacy of a private discussion, as in other Zen schools *(dokusan)* but in the Dojo, so that the whole sangha can benefit.

Mu – Japanese. A prefix meaning "nothing," "nothingness," "none." Nothing, but not in the sense of a nothing that opposes something. More than a negation, *mu* holds a connotation of absence. It is found in many Zen expressions.

Muga – Japanese. (Sanskrit, *anatman*.) Non-self, absence of ego. The principle of not identifying with ego as a separate existence and the individuality of the soul.

Mushin – Japanese. Non–mind. Without personal consciousness. A state of consciousness with no dualistic thought, the end of discriminating thought, the mind that doesn't fixate.

Mushotoku – Japanese. Without wishing for gain, without goal, *Mushotoku* refers to a practice without objective, without a goal. The fact of giving or acting without expecting a result.

Nagarjuna – (2nd to 3rd century) Indian Buddhist philosopher, founder of the Madyamika or "Middle Way" school and the fourteenth patriarch of Zen Buddhism, after the historical Buddha. Famed for his teachings on the doctrine of *ku* (in Sanskrit, *sunnyata*, emptiness) which he developed from study of the *Pranjaparamita* sutras.

Naraka – Sanskrit. Hell.

Narita Roshi – Disciple of Kodo Sawaki who came from Japan to join Master Deshimaru at Val d'Isère.

Nembutsu – Japanese. Invocation of the name of Amitabha Buddha, recited out loud, or a prayer which replaces meditation in the Tendai and Shin Buddhist schools.

Nirvana – Sanskrit. Complete extinction of phenomena. Supreme wisdom. Liberation from the cycle of rebirth and from karma. Sometimes synonymous with death.

Glossary

Nirvana (Sutra of) – (Japanese, *Nehangyo.*) Sutras of Shakyamuni Buddha brought out just before his death, describing the events linked to his entry into nirvana. They emphasize the true nature of the Self and the eternal presence of the state of buddha in all things.

Nyojo – Japanese. (Chinese, Tiantong Rujing, 1163-1228). Disciple of Setcho Chikan and the master of Dogen. Soto master of the Sung Dynasty who was installed as abbot of Tendo monastery in South China and taught only zazen. A firm adversary of "spiritual syncretism" he concluded that Bodhidharma's unique teaching had need of neither amalgamation nor addition. Nyojo was the last of the great Chinese *Ch'an* masters. And it is thanks to Dogen, who was his disciple, that his teaching has been continued until today.

Obaku – Japanese. (Chinese, Huang-po, died 850.) Disciple of Hyakujo and the master of Rinzai. One of the great masters of Tang China. "An ancient Buddha beyond time," Dogen said of him.

Rakusu – Japanese. Small five-band *kesa* worn around the neck both within and outside of the practice place. In contrast to the large *kesa* reserved for monks and nuns, the *rakusu* can be worn by people who have received Bodhisattva ordination.

Rensaku – Japanese. Series of *kyosaku* strikes given by the master or an assistant on the muscles between the shoulder and nape of the neck. Used to restore the concentration of the whole sangha when a serious mistake has been committed.

Rinzai – Japanese. (School.) Founded by Master Rinzai in 9th-century China. Now the main school of Zen together with the Soto school. In Rinzai, *koans* are used more formally and zazen, practiced facing the centre of the Dojo, is seen as a method to attain Satori.

Rinzai – Japanese. (Chinese, Lin-chi, died 866.) Zen master, disciple of Obaku. To train his disciples, Rinzai would use methods intended to overturn ordinary consciousness such as a rough shout "Ho!" and sudden blows with a stick (*shippei, kyosaku*) or fly-whisk (*hossu*).

Rishu kyo – Japanese. Sutra glorifying sex which praises the original instinct of the human being.

Samadhi – Sanskrit. (Japanese, *zanmai*). State of meditation and receptive awareness during zazen. Pure attention, unconscious and without object. Master Dogen said: "The samadhi of Buddhas and patriarchs is frost and hail, wind and lightening."

Samsara – Sanskrit. (Japanese, *shoji*.) Cycle of transmigration of the soul and of existences (birth, death, rebirth) conditioned by attachment. The opposite of nirvana, even though fundamentally they are not separate. Consisting of six worlds of possible existence, which are in fact states of mind: *shomon* (human), *asura* (warrior), *deva* (god), *chikuso* (animal), *gaki* (hungry spirit), *naraka* (hell realms).

Samu – Japanese. Period of collective work dedicated to maintenance, cooking, etc.

Sandokai – Japanese. "Fusion of difference and similarity." A poem by Master Sekito Kisen (700–790). One of the fundamental Zen texts, finishing with the famous verse: "You who seek the Way, I implore you not to lose the present moment."

Sanpai – Japanese. Series of three prostrations, the forehead touching the ground and the palms of the hands raised.

Sanran – Japanese. State of mental agitation and nervous tension during the practice of zazen.

Glossary

Satori – Japanese. Enlightenment or awakening. Not a special state of consciousness, but rather the return to the normal condition, to the original nature. In the Rinzai school, Satori is the successful conclusion of fruitful practice and the object of a relentless search. In the Soto school, practice itself is Satori, meaning the realization of our true nature.

Sariputra – Sanskrit. Close disciple of Shakyamuni Buddha.

Sawaki, Kodo (1880–1965) – Japanese Zen master, and the master of Taisen Deshimaru. Ordained by Sawada Koho at the age of eighteen, he studied with Shokoku Zenko. He spent most of his life outside temples, travelling around Japan to spread the practice of zazen, which earned him the nickname of "Homeless Kodo."

Sekito – Japanese. (Chinese, Che-t'e or Si-k'ien, 700–790.) "Stone Head." Disciple of Seigen and the master of Yakusan. Considered to be the first link of the Soto Zen lineage. Author of *Sandokai,* one of the fundamental texts. A poem says: "To the west of the river lived Baso / To the south of the lake, Sekito. Men go from one to the other / Those who have not met them live in ignorance.

Sensei – Japanese. Teacher. Everyday Japanese term used by students to address their teachers. Master Deshimaru preferred to be called this rather than *roshi*.

Sesshin – Japanese. "To touch the mind." A time of collective retreat of several days dedicated to the intensive practice of zazen, interspersed with samu.

Shakyamuni – Sanskrit. "The sage of the Shakya." The historical Buddha.

Shastra – Japanese. Commentary on a sutra.

Shiho – Japanese. This term relates to two very different concepts. 1) Originally, it was the intimate understanding, from "heart-mind to heart-mind," between master and disciple. 2) Within the institution of Japanese Zen, it is the certificate which authorizes the monk to teach.

Shikantaza – Japanese. Simply sitting. Seated concentration in zazen posture.

Shiki – Japanese. See *ku*.

Shin Jin Mei – Japanese. "Poem of faith in mind" by Master Sosan, the third patriarch. Composed in the 7th century CE, this is one of the most ancient *Ch'an* texts transmitted within Zen. It affirms above all the faith in mind having left behind dualistic tendencies.

Shobogenzo – Japanese. "The Treasure of the eye of the true Law" traditionally seen as the teaching transmitted by the Buddha, outside the scriptures. Within Soto Zen this refers to Master Dogen's major work, partly compiled by his disciple Ejo, and the first important Buddhist writing in Japanese.

Sotoshu – Japanese. The school of Soto Zen.

Sotoshu shumusho – Japanese. Administrative office of the Soto school based in Tokyo. Among Soto school *sanghas,* some follow its rules and others do not.

Sutra – Sanskrit. (Japanese, *Kyo* or *Gyo.*) Sermons given by the Buddha. According to tradition, they were recalled from memory by his disciple Ananda at the time of the First Buddhist Council which met in 480 BCE, just after the death of Shakyamuni.

Suzuki D.T. (1870–1966) – Buddhist scholar, translator and disseminator of Zen in the West. Skilled in the *koan* method, he studied Zen following Shaku Soen and Sokatsu Shaku, who asked him to translate Zen texts into English for an educated readership.

Suzuki Shunryu (1904–1971) – Monk of the Soto Zen school, endorsed by the Sotoshu Shumucho, who arrived in the U.S. in 1959 and founded the San Francisco Zen Center and the Tassajara Zen Mountain Center, the first temple outside Asia.

Tenzo - Japanese. Head cook. Master of the kitchens.

Uji – Japanese, "being-time." One of the chapters of Master Dogen's *Shobogenzo,* written in 1240.

Unsui – Japanese. Literally "water-cloud." Expression used to describe the Zen monk, who, like the clouds and the water of the river, attaches himself to nothing whatever.

Vimalakirti – Sanskrit. "Renowned Immaculate." A lay disciple of the Buddha whose understanding surpassed that of the monks. According to the Great Vehicle text which bears his name, he was an incredible scholar.

Way – (Chinese, *tao* or *dao.*) Cosmic order, or the path, the practice in harmony with the cosmic order. The Way of Buddha or *butsu-do.*

Zafu – Japanese. Round cushion filled with kapok on which one sits to practice zazen.

Zazen – Japanese. (Chinese, *T'so chan.*) The syllable *za* means "to be seated." To sit with legs crossed, in lotus or half-lotus, on a zafu facing the wall.

Zen – Japanese. Abbreviation of the word *zenna,* a Japanese transcription of the Chinese term *chan'na,* itself derived from the Sanskrit *dhyana,* meaning concentration of the mind or attention. A branch of Mahayana Buddhism, introduced to Japan by Masters Eisai and Dogen in the 13th century.

Zeisler – Étienne Mokusho. (French, 1943–1990.) One of the closest disciples of Master Deshimaru and his interpreter.

INDEX

A —
Action, xix, 8, 28, 73, 82ff, 96
Aksara, 81
Alan Watts Zen, 140
Amida Buddha, 99
Amida Buddha Sutra, 158
Asceticism, 50
Asura /*Asura Zen*, 135
Atman, 57
Attachment, 5, 10, 22ff, 166; *see also* Bonno
Augustine, Saint, 127
Avidya, 40

B —
Behaviorism, 37, 74ff, 108
Biran, Maine de, 92
Bodhi, 161, 175 (Glossary)
Bodhidharma, xxiv, 51, 175 (Glossary)
Bodhisattva, 18, 70, 112, 175, 181(Glossary)
Bonno, 4ff, 8, 50, 67ff, 97, 175 (Glossary)
Breathing, in zazen, xxiii, 33, 115
Buddha, xxiii, 21ff, 29, 51, 53ff, 163, 175 (Glossary)
  Shakyamuni, 5, 185 (Glossary)
Buddhism 37, 74, 84, 88, 93, 166, 176 (Glossary)
  in China, 101, 104, 175 (Glossary)
  and Christianity, 8, 98ff
  Hinayana, 48, 178 (Glossary)
  Indian, 78, 102, 104
  Japanese, 109
  Mahayana, 48, 66ff, 97, 104, 181 (Glossary)
  Tantric, 26, 50
  Tibetan, 26

C —
Catholicism, 56, 129
Causality, 38ff, 44ff, 74, 179 (Glossary)
Cause and effect, 22, 38, 48, 102, 179 (Glossary)
Ceremony, 74, 126
Christ, 132ff, 141, 145, 149, 152, 157
Christianity, 8, 26, 99, 111, 166
Contagious action, 73ff
Cosmic
  energy, 12, 63
  existentialism, 93
  order, 94, 115, 122, 130, 155ff
  power, 3ff, 8, 26ff, 43, 48

D —
Daichi, Master, 96, 125, 176 (Glossary)
Death, fear of, 122
Descartes, 4ff, 92
Destiny, 29, 33ff
Determinism, 30, 171
Dharma, 93, 176
Dogen, 17, 19, 96, 105ff, 137ff, 160ff, 176 (Glossary)

E —
Eckhart, Meister, 127, 129ff
Effect, *see* Cause and effect
Ego, 12, 19, 23, 25ff, 43, 66ff, 94
Eido, Master, 141
Eihei-ji, Temple of, 164, 176 (Glossary)

189

Index

Einstein, 163
Eno, 85, 177
Eternity, 37, 50, 52, 58, 162
European philosophy, 29, 39
Evil, *see* Good and bad
Existentialism, 93

F —
Fatalism, 33ff, 48, 171
Freedom, 37, 46, 122, 132
Fukanzazengi, 3, 19, 160, 177 (Glossary)

G —
Gassho, 121, 130, 147, 177
Genjo koan, 18, 26, 177; *see also* Shobogenzo
God, 26, 115, 127, 129ff, 146, 149, 150, 152, 163
Godo, 123, 177 (Glossary)
Good and bad, 6, 8, 23
Greek, mythology, 34, 35

H —
Hannya shingyo, Sutra, 66, 98, 110, 126
  definition, 178 (Glossary)
Happiness, 7, 30, 120
Heidegger, 161, 163
Hesse, Herman, 35
Hinayana, buddhism, 48, 178 (Glossary)
Hinduism, 22, 178
Hishiryo, 3, 17, 55, 65, 178 (Glossary)
  consciousness, 6, 27, 57
Hokyo zanmai, 10
Homer, 35
Humanism, 29, 78
Hypothalamus, 65

I —
I Shin den Shin, 32, 38, 179 (Glossary)
Immortality of the soul, 56
Impermanence, doctrine of, 78
Infectious, action, 73
Innen, 44, 179 (Glossary)
Interdependence, 39-45

K —
Kai, 102, 109
Kaijo, 18, 71, 179 (Glossary)
Kant, Emmanuel, 56
Karma, xix, 8, 12, 52, 179
  and causality, 81ff
  changing, 171ff
  and the cosmos, 21ff
  cutting the roots of, 88ff, 94ff
  destiny and, 33ff
  interdependence and, 43ff
  karmic effects, 73ff
  non-manifested, 83ff, 91ff
  observing one's, 110ff
  repeats itself, 118f
  without substance, 27f
Keisei sanshoku, xv
Kensho, 54, 129, 137
Keyserling, 36
Ki, 33, 44f, 53f, 151, 180 (Glossary)
Kinhin, 93, 105, 116f, 128, 153, 155, 180 (Glossary)
Koan, 17, 47, 120, 180
Kodo Sawaki, xx, 48, 100f, 164, 167f, 185 (Glossary)
Ksara, 81
Ku, 25f, 66ff, 101, 180
Ku soku ze shiki, 25, 44, 66, 110f, 161, 180 (Glossary)
Kyosaku, 7, 38, 71f, 80, 100, 121ff, 181 (Glossary)

L —
Lorenz, Konrad, 65, 74
Love, 18, 130, 166

M —
Mahayana, Buddhism, 66, 104, 181 (Glossary)
Meditation, 63ff,
Meister Eckhart, 127, 129f
Mendel, law of, 155
Merleau, Ponty, 74
Milinda, King, 11, 24, 56
Moral, judgment, 23f, 75f, 81
Mu, 27, 101f, 182
Mu ge ko, 165
Muga, 25, 104, 109, 111, 182 (Glossary)
Mushin, 27, 182
Mushogo, 84f, 87; *see also* Nonmanifest karma
Mushotoku, 43, 129ff, 182 (Glossary)

N —
Nagarjuna, 51, 182
Nagasena, Bodhisattva, 11, 24, 56f
Naraka, 5, 136
Naraka Zen, 134
Narita Roshi, 10, 20
Nembutsu, 71, 96, 98, 101, 109
Nietzsche, 36
Nirvana, 47, 67, 102
　absolute, 68
　living, 48, 50ff, 55, 58f, 68f, 90, 104
Non-thinking, *see* Hishiryo
Nyojo, Master, 107, 137f

O —
Obaku, Zen, 96, 137

P —
Pascal, 92
Passion, 4, 30, 5
Patriarchs
　First, 51; *see also* Bodhidharma
　Second, 145; *see also* Eka
　Third, 124; *see also* Sosan
　Fifth, *see* Konin
　Sixth, 85; *see also* Eno
　Fourteenth, in Buddha's lineage; *see* Nagarajuna, 51
Pavlov, 74
Pope, the 64, 128

R —
Rakusu, 18, *see also* Kesa
Reincarnation, 9f, 24, 27, 102, 104
Rinzai, Zen, 47, 100, 120, 137, 182 (Glossary)

S —
Saint Augustine, 127
Sampai, 98
Samsara, 10f, 88, 102
Sandokai, 10, 91
Satori, 18, 23, 68, 69, 97, 120, 140, 166f, 185 (Glossary)
　certification of, 47, 53f
Sesshin, 32, 115, 117f, 152, 185 (Glossary)
Sex, 30, 37, 50, 135
Shakti, 26, 27, 73
　infinity of, 102
Shakyamuni Buddha, *see* Buddha Shakyamuni
Shiho, 32, 47
Shikantaza, 17, 74, 107, 125, 186 (Glossary)
Shiki soku ze ku, 25, 44, 66, 110ff, 161; *see also* Ku soku ze shiki
Shin jin datsu raku, 30, 138
Shin Jin Mei, 27, 124, 186 (Glossary)
Shinran, 96, 101

Index

Shobogenzo, 82, 96, 161, 186 (Glossary)
Shodoka, 10, 163
Socrates, 81
Soto Zen, 19, 47, 111, 129, 138
   founder of, *see* Dogen
   Rinzai and, 129
Sotoba, 5, 79
Soul, 55ff, 129
Suffering, 93, 97
Suicide, 122
Suzuki, D.T., 156f, 186 (Glossary)
Suzuki Shunryu Roshi, 187 (Glossary)

T —
Tantric Buddhism, 26, 52, 55
Tantrism, sexual, 52
Théravada, *see* Hinayana.
Time, three notions of, 161f
Transmigration, 9ff, 21ff, 102ff

W —
Watts, Alan, 6, 140
Willpower, 3f, 45, 84

Y —
Yamada, Zenji Reirin, xxvi,
Yoka Daishi, xxiv; *see also* Shodoka

Z —
Zazen, xxii, 3, 17ff, 32f, 47, 57ff, 63ff, 85ff, 115ff, 163f, 187 (Glossary)
"Zazen," poem, 17
Zen
   Obaku, xxiv, 96, 137, 183 (Glossary)
   Rinzai, xxiv, 47, 120, 129, 137, 183 (Glossary)
   Soto, xxvi, 47, 101, 129, 183 (Glossary)

OTHER ENGLISH-LANGUAGE BOOKS BY ROSHI TAISEN DESHIMARU

The Voice of the Valley, edited by Philippe Coupey, Bobbs-Merrill (1979) Out of Print
The Ring of the Way, with Evelyn de Smedt, Dutton (1987) Out of Print
Questions to a Zen Master, Political and Spiritual Answers from Mokudo Taisen Deshimaru, Penguin (1991) Out of Print
The Zen Way to the Martial Arts, Penguin (1992)
Sit, edited by Philippe Coupey, Hohm Press (1996)
The Way of True Zen, American Zen Association (2002)
The Sutra of Great Wisdom, on the Hannya Haramita Shingyo, revised by Philippe Coupey, Edition Integrale, AZI (2007)
Mushotoku Mind, The Heart of the Heart Sutra, edited by Richard Collins, Hohm Press (2012)
Zen and Budo, revised by Philippe Coupey, bilingual book English/French, Budo Editions (2013)

OTHER ENGLISH-LANGUAGE BOOKS BY PHILIPPE REI RYU COUPEY

Current Zen Titles:
The Song of the Wind in the Dry Tree, Commentaries on Dogen's Sansho Doei *and Koun Ejo's* Komyozo Zanmai, Hohm Press (2014)
Zen Simply Sitting, A Monk's Commentary on the Fukanzazengi by Master Dogen, Hohm Press, (2007)
In the Belly of the Dragon, The Shinjinmei *by Master Sosan*, Vol. 1, American Zen Association New Orleans, (2005)

Upcoming:
In the Belly of the Dragon, The Shinjinmei *by Master Sosan,* Vol. 1. revised version
In the Belly of the Dragon The Shinjinmei *by Master Sosan,* Vol. 2
Zen Today, Teachings on Different Subjects

Fiction Titles:
Horse Medicine, American Zen Association, New Orleans, 2002. Alias, M. C. Dalley
Temple Rapidly Vanishing, Deux Versants Éditeur, 2012, Alias, M. C. Dalley

OTHER TITLES OF INTEREST FROM HOHM PRESS

ZEN, SIMPLY SITTING
A Zen Monk's Commentary on the Fukanzazengi by Master Dogen
by Philippe Coupey

No diluted, dumbed-down or sugarcoated version of Zen teaching and practice will be found here. Long-time Zen teacher Philippe Coupey offers readers a fresh, sometimes irreverent perspective of an ancient classic, the *Fukanzazengi*, a short basic text on how to practice zazen written by Master Dogen in 1227. Coupey's approach to this timeless teaching is based on the work of his own distinguished master, Taisen Deshimaru, the Japanese Soto Zen teacher who brought Zen to Europe.

Paper, 120 pages, $14.95   ISBN: 978-1-890772-61-1

• • •

SIT
Zen Teachings of Master Taisen Deshimaru
edited by Philippe Coupey

"To understand oneself is to understand the universe."
—Taisen Deshimaru Roshi

Like spending a month in retreat with a great Zen master. SIT addresses the practice of meditation for both beginners and long-time students of Zen. Deshimaru's powerful and insightful approach is particularly suited to those who desire an experience of the rigorous Soto tradition in a form that is accessible to Westerners.

Paper, 375 pages, photographs, $8.50   ISBN: 978-0-934252-61-4
(publisher's "Seconds" only)

To Order: 800-381-2700, or visit our website, www.hohmpress.com

OTHER TITLES OF INTEREST FROM HOHM PRESS

THE SONG OF THE WIND IN THE DRY TREE
Commentaries on Dogen's *Sansho Doei* and
Koun Ejo's *Komyozo Zanmai*
by Rei Ryu Philippe Coupey

This book of commentaries covers two 13th-century Japanese texts. In Part I, Coupey has chosen twelve poems from the *Sansho Doei*, a collection composed by Master Dogen Zenji between 1245-1253. In Part II, he comments on the complete text of *Komyozo Zanmai* (1278) by Dogen's disciple and successor, Master Koun Ejo. The author's fresh interpretation of these two classic texts rests on an intimate and fundamental experience with this material. His words are addressed to the reader's heart, shedding light on our own quest and ratifying the discoveries that we may have made along the way.

Paper, $12.95, 80 pages   ISBN: 978-1-935387-82-4

• • •

NO FEAR ZEN
Discovering Balance in an Unbalanced World
by Richard Collins

The brief Zen talks that constitute the core of the book continue the tradition of spontaneous oral teachings delivered by the teacher (or roshi) during zazen. *No Fear Zen* presents an approach to Zen practice that focuses on concentration and sitting (*shikantaza*) as a discipline that can be practiced in everyday life with the dedication of the samurai. This book contends that compassion and mindfulness occur naturally, spontaneously, and automatically from right practice without any goal or object whatsoever.

Paper, $21.95, 264 pages   ISBN: 978-1-935387-95-4

To Order: 800-381-2700, or visit our website, www.hohmpress.com

OTHER TITLES OF INTEREST FROM HOHM PRESS

MUSHOTOKU MIND
The Heart of the Heart Sutra
by Taisen Deshimaru
Edited by Richard Collins

"*Mushotoku* mind" means an attitude of no profit, no gain. It is the core of master Taisen Deshimaru's Zen. This respected teacher of Japanese Soto Zen moved from Japan in 1967 and brought this work to Paris, from where it was disseminated throughout the West. This book presents his commentary on the most renowned of Buddhist texts, the *Heart Sutra,* known in Japanese as *Hannya Shingyo*—a philosophical investigation on the futility of philosophical investigation.

Paper, 176 pages, $16.95   ISBN: 978-1-935387-27-5

• • •

JOURNEY TO HEAVENLY MOUNTAIN
An American's Pilgrimage to the Heart of Buddhism in Modern China
by Jay Martin

"I came to China to live in Buddhist monasteries and to revisit my soul," writes best-selling American author and distinguished scholar Jay Martin of his 1998 pilgrimage. This book is an account of one man's spiritual journey. His intention? To penetrate the soul of China and its wisdom. *Journey to Heavenly Mountain* is about the author's desire to know God and sacred things; his yearning for illuminated insight and his hunger to achieve virtue and calmness of spirit. Martin focuses on the profound richness and varieties of inner life, along with the potential for growth in wisdom and empathy which life among these dedicated Buddhists offered.

"Well-written and intelligent, it will appeal to both casual readers and to specialists." —**Library Journal**

Paper, 264 pages, $16.95   ISBN: 978-1-1-890772-17-8

To Order: 800-381-2700, or visit our website, www.hohmpress.com

OTHER TITLES OF INTEREST FROM HOHM PRESS

FEAST OR FAMINE
Teaching on Mind and Emotions
by Lee Lozowick

This book focuses on core issues related to human suffering: the mind that doesn't "Know Thyself," and the emotions that create terrifying imbalance and unhappiness. The author, a spiritual teacher for over 35 years, details the working of mind and emotions, offering practical interventions for when they are raging out of control. A practical handbook for meditators and anyone dedicated to "work on self." Lee Lozowick has written over twenty books, including: *Conscious Parenting; The Alchemy of Transformation;* and *The Alchemy of Love and Sex*; and has been translated and published in French, German, Spanish, Portuguese and other languages.

Paper, 256 pages, $19.95   ISBN: 978-1-890772-79-6

• • •

ZEN TRASH
The Irreverent and Sacred Teaching Stories of Lee Lozowick
Edited and with Commentary by Sylvan Incao

This book contains dozens of teaching stories from many world religious traditions—including Zen, Christianity, Tibetan Buddhism, Sufism and Hinduism—rendered with a twist of humor, irony or provocation by contemporary Western Baul spiritual teacher Lee Lozowick. They are compiled from twenty-five years of Lozowick's talks and seminars in the U.S., Canada, Europe, Mexico and India. These stories will typically confound the mind and challenge any conventional seriousness about the spiritual path. In essence, however, they hold what every traditional teaching story has always held¾the possibility of glimpsing reality, beyond the multiple illusions that surround the truth.

Paper, 156 pages, $12.95   ISBN: 978-1-890772-21-5

To Order: 800-381-2700, or visit our website, www.hohmpress.com

OTHER TITLES OF INTEREST FROM HOHM PRESS

SELF OBSERVATION ~ THE AWAKENING OF CONSCIENCE
An Owner's Manual
by Red Hawk

This book is an in-depth examination of the much needed process of "self" study known as self observation. It offers the most direct, non-pharmaceutical means of healing the attention dysfunction which plagues contemporary culture. Self observation, the author asserts, is the most ancient, scientific, and proven means to develop conscience, this crucial inner guide to awakening and a moral life.

This book is for the lay reader, both the beginner and the advanced student of self observation. No other book on the market examines this practice in such detail. There are hundreds of books on self-help and meditation, but almost none on self-study via self observation, and none with the depth of analysis, wealth of explication, and richness of experience that this book offers.

Paper, 160 pages, $14.95   ISBN: 978-1-890772-92-5

• • •

AS ONE IS
To Free the Mind from All Conditioning
by J. Krishnamurti

In this series of previously unpublished lectures, Krishnamurti examines a world in which booming productivity and scientific advancement *should* promise a happy future, but don't. He asks his listeners to consider that we are merely substituting comfortable myths for our fears, and living as if these myths were true. The author patiently explains how to examine our assumptions; how to question our "conditioned" beliefs, and ultimately how to listen for truth…both within and from the world around us. *As One Is* offers readers a rare opportunity to gain greater self-understanding, and clarity in the midst of confusion. Krishnamurti offers a means to transform thinking and hence our relationship to life.

"I know of no other living man whose thought is more inspiring."
— Henry Miller

Paper, 120 pages, $14.95   ISBN: 978-1-890772-62-8

To Order: 800-381-2700, or visit our website, www.hohmpress.com

About the Author

Taisen Deshimaru

Mokudo Taisen Deshimaru has been called "the modern-day Bodhidharma" because of his formidable character, his uncompromising Zen practice and his pioneering mission to plant the seed of authentic Zen in a new land (in this case, Europe).

He was born Yasuo Deshimaru on November 20, 1914 in a small village near Saga. His mother was a fervent Buddhist, his father a businessman. The polarity of their worldviews made a mark on the boy, who from a very young age considered it his destiny to resolve the contradiction between the spiritual and the material.

He met his master Kodo Sawaki when he was eighteen and began sitting zazen with him two years later. He saw the master regularly while continuing his life as a businessman and, later, a husband and father of three. Over time, he became his disciple, and an intimate relationship unfolded naturally between them over a span of thirty years.

A year after Sawaki's death, Deshimaru went to Paris in 1967 alone, with no money, no French. He had secured an invitation from a macrobiotic group, and lived in the back room of a health-food store, practicing zazen every day and surviving by giving massages. Slowly, people began sitting with him, and his reputation grew. As word spread that a real Zen master was living on the rue Pernety, more and more people came to practice with him. He opened his first dojo in Paris in 1972, and began giving ordinations and leading sesshin all over Europe.

He pursued his mission with a prodigious, unflagging energy, always seeking to reconcile tradition and modernity, science and spirituality, East and West, and always returning to the essence of the teaching he received from his master. He had exceptional charisma, a great simplicity mixed with a sense of humor, which attracted not only disciples, but also some of the most intriguing scientists, artists, philosophers and politicians of his time.

Deshimaru's close sangha consisted largely of free-thinking young people who were not always easily disciplined, but who were full of an unbridled enthusiasm and the vastness of beginner's mind. Together they published books, organized sesshin and summer retreats and opened more than a hundred Zen centers.

He was diagnosed with cancer in early 1982, though he continued to practice with his disciples through the spring. His last words before returning to Japan for medical treatment were, "Please, continue zazen." He died there on April 30, 1982.

About the Editor

Philippe Rei Ryu Coupey, born and raised in New York City, is a Soto Zen teacher in the lineage of Kodo Sawaki. He met Master Deshimaru in 1972 and followed him as a close disciple. Having studied literature at the Sorbonne, he worked with Deshimaru on the latter's teaching. Three books came out of this collaboration, including this current volume. Today, after forty years of Zen practice, Coupey directs a large community of practitioners in Europe, in a lineage directly transmitted from master to disciple. The practice is shikantaza: simply sitting, without goal or profitseeking mind.

Contact Information: Association Zen Sans demeure, 6 square de Port Royal, 75013 Paris, France; email: ohnebleibe@gmail.com website: www.zen-road.org

About Hohm Press

Hohm Press is committed to publishing books that provide readers with alternatives to the materialistic values of the current culture, and promote self-awareness, the recognition of interdependence, and compassion. Our subject areas include parenting, transpersonal psychology, religious studies, women's studies, the arts and poetry.

Contact Information: Hohm Press, PO Box 4410, Chino Valley, Arizona, 86323, USA; 800-381-2700, or 928-636-3331; email: hppublisher@cableone.net

Visit our website at www.hohmpress.com